Holding Fast the Faithful Word

Episcopacy and the Office of the Holy Ministry in the Evangelical Lutheran Diocese of North America

Three Essays

Rev. John Rutowicz
Pastor, St. Boniface Lutheran Church
Niles, Michigan

Published with Four Appendices:
The ELDoNA Charter
The Niles Theses
The Malone Theses
The Rite of Consecration to the Office of Bishop

Repristination Press
Malone, Texas

June 2013

Repristination Press
716 HCR 3424 E
Malone, Texas 76660

ISBN 1-891469-46-0

Table of Contents

Foreword

It is a profound pleasure to write a few words of introduction to this volume of essays written by one of the founding pastors of the ELDoNA. Fr. John Rutowicz and I met while we were both seminarians, and I have had the opportunity to watch him develop into a fine scholar and faithful pastor in the service of Christ's Church. Fr. Rutowicz has been a good friend for many years, and I treasure the counsel which he has offered on many occasions.

I am writing this brief introduction only a few days after the seventh anniversary of the founding of the Evangelical Lutheran Diocese of North America (ELDoNA). As noted above, Fr. Rutowicz is one of the founding members of the diocese; what is not as widely known is that he suggested the name of the diocese and led the initial discussion of its episcopal structure. The three essays included in this book were profoundly helpful in discussions of the episcopate with those who were not of our fellowship. However, even more importantly, Fr. Rutowicz helped guide our diocesan discussions of the episcopate, and played a fundamental role in shaping the rite of consecration which was used in 2010.

The three essays are not 'official' doctrinal statements of the diocese regarding the episcopate; they are, however, documents which have been appreciated throughout the ELDoNA for the insights offered therein. It is our hope that through this publication, those who are not familiar with the episcopal office—or who labor under medieval notions of that office—would gain a better understanding of the reforms of this office set forth in the Lutheran Confessions, and the expression of those reforms implemented within our diocese.

Rt. Rev. James D. Heiser
Bishop, The Evangelical Lutheran Diocese of North America
Thursday after Trinity 2, A.D. 2013

An Apology for Episcopacy*

Episcopal polity is not the only option that is open to Lutherans, but I would suggest that it is the best option. It is an important component in the well-being (*bene esse*) of the Church. With the founding of the Evangelical Lutheran Diocese of North America on June 6, 2006, we are seeing an evangelical episcopacy reestablished among confessional Lutherans in America. One can think of the abortive attempts among confessional Lutherans (for example, Martin Stephan) and non-orthodox groups such as the ELCA call their leaders bishops, but one can hardly think of the ELCA as Church in anything but sociological terms. However, a truly orthodox Lutheran body, which maintains the historic three-fold office of the ministry is, to the best of my knowledge, something that has not been seen yet in our country. I pray that with the founding of the ELDoNA, and the calling of her first bishop, James D. Heiser, the wedding of confessional faithfulness and episcopacy will be blessed by our Lord with long life.

THE SCRIPTURES AND POLITY

Lutherans clearly teach that there is only one office in the Church, the office of the ministry. There are not two or three different divinely established offices in the New Testament Church. A ranking of clergy (deacons/presbyters/bishops) is simply by human arrangement. While it is clear that

* Presented at the Theological Colloquium of The Evangelical Lutheran Diocese of North America (29 August 2007).

in the New Testament the terms for bishop and presbyter (or, "elder") are interchangeable, there does seem to be a precedent for episcopal oversight among members of the office of the ministry. James, the cousin of our Lord, seems to have a bishop-like position in the Jerusalem Church. James also certainly seems to have a prominent position at the council of Jerusalem in Acts 15. Further, he seems to have a prominent position with regard to the other "elders" in Acts 21:18. Was James a "bishop" as we think of them? Probably not with all the ideas that we bring to the term, but an office of oversight does seem to be implied.

There are other men mentioned in Holy Scripture besides James who have this episcopal function. At times, both Timothy and Titus seemed to function as bishops in the New Testament. First, Timothy was charged by the Apostle Paul, "stay there in Ephesus so that you may command certain men not to teach false doctrines any longer..." (1 Tim. 1:3). Timothy is to "command" those who teach God's people: This is doctrinal discipline, and Timothy is carrying it out with regard to what seems to be clergy. Second, Timothy also seems to be put in the position of judge when questions of impropriety surfaced. St. Paul instructs Timothy, "Do not entertain an accusation against an elder unless it is brought by two or three witnesses" (1 Tim. 5:19). Timothy was in a position of judging over other "elders," which in the New Testament refers to clergy. Third, Timothy also seems to have been responsible for appointing other clergy in the Church. "And the things you have heard me say in the presence of many witnesses entrust to reliable men who will also be qualified to teach others" (2 Tim. 2:2).

Titus also seems to perform episcopal functions. St. Paul tells him, "The reason I left you in Crete was that you might straighten out what was left unfinished and appoint elders in every town, as I directed you" (Tit. 1:5). Now, these passages are not commands by our Lord for episcopal polity: they are simply instructions from the Apostle Paul to his apprentices or descriptions of life in the earliest Church.

A description of how the Church was arranged in the Greek world is found in Acts. Paul and Barnabas appointed clergy: "Paul and Barnabas appointed elders for them in each church and, with prayer and fasting, committed them to the Lord, in whom they had put their trust" (Acts 14:23). Many Christians argue over the significance of these and other passages. Christians come to different conclusions over the witness of the biblical record, usually finding in that record more to support their particular position than is warranted. But it can be said that while there is no command to adopt episcopal polity in the New Testament, there is precedent for a type of episcopacy in the New Testament. To interpret these passages as depicting a type of episcopacy is, probably, the best interpretation of them. They demonstrate primitive episcopacy in action. This argument—that is, that they depict a primitive episcopacy—is strengthened by the fact that episcopal polity is found to be nearly universal very shortly after the apostolic era. And so, while episcopacy is simply a human arrangement in the Church, it seems to have been the normal arrangement since the New Testament itself.

THE LUTHERAN CONFESSIONS AND POLITY

Since episcopal polity is a thing that is neither commanded nor forbidden in the Bible, Lutherans can have other arrangements. But what is even more compelling than the biblical argument with regard to episcopacy is the position taken by the Lutheran Confessions themselves. While church structure (or polity) is 'free' (that is, not a matter which is divinely-commanded) for Lutherans, it is by no means something that is unimportant. As a matter of fact,

Philip Melanchthon (with Luther's approval) expressed a very definite opinion with regard to episcopacy in the Apology of the Augsburg Confession. He said,

> On this matter [church order] we have given frequent testimony in the assembly to our deep desire to maintain the church polity and various ranks of the ecclesiastical hierarchy, although they were created by human authority. ... Thus the cruelty of the bishops is the reason for the abolition of canonical government in some places, despite our earnest desire to keep it. ... Furthermore, we want at this point to declare our willingness to keep the ecclesiastical and canonical polity, provided that the bishops stop raging against our churches. This willingness will be our defense, both before God and among all nations, present and future, against the charge that we have undermined the authority of the bishops. (Apology XIV).

When Melanchthon says that the Lutherans desire to keep the polity and hierarchy of the Church, he is naturally referring to the only polity and hierarchy which existed at that time: the Roman Catholic polity and hierarchy. It might come as a shock to many Lutherans to learn that it was Luther's and Melanchthon's "deep desire," and "earnest desire" (to quote the Apology) to keep the hierarchy and polity of episcopacy. And this desire of the Lutheran confessors was not something that was limited or conditioned to the sixteenth century. Melanchthon says that this "deep desire," this "willingness" would be their defense against charges of an anti-episcopal attitude for both the "present and future." In the light of the very strong language employed by Melanchthon in Article XIV of the Apology, it is amazing that the confessional churches of the old Synodical Conference did not form themselves as episcopacies, nor did they appear to have ever seriously considered becoming episcopally-ordered.

Article XIV is not the only place episcopacy is addressed. Even beyond the above quotation of Article XIV of the Apology, the Lutheran Confessions simply assume episcopacy to be the norm in the Church. Article XXVIII of both the Augsburg Confession and the Apology, and part of the Treatise, talk about the proper role of bishops. This sort of discussion is only appropriate if one assumes an episcopal structure.

THE WITNESS OF THE CHURCH'S LIFE AND HISTORY TO POLITY

Episcopacy also has the weight of history behind it. One of the most important arguments for episcopacy is its early and nearly universal appearance in the life of the Christian Church. This would lead one to believe that it was not some movement of a particular group in the Church, but, in fact, it was the normal development of the structure of the apostolic church. By the time of St. Ignatius (circa A.D. 110), there was a three-fold ministry in existence in Asia minor (that is, present day Turkey). By the end of the second century, episcopacy is attested to by Irenaeus and Tertullian in Gaul (France) and Africa. There was an episcopacy in Rome by the middle of the second century.[*] In defending the concept of apostolic succession in Rome, St. Irenaeus said, "The blessed apostles, then, having founded and built up the Church, committed into the hands of Linus the office of the episcopate."[†] One does not have to accept Irenaeus' arguments about apostolic succession nor the primacy of the pope to acknowledge the fact of the existence of the office of bishop in the Church well before A.D. 180 when Irenaeus

* Ivar Asheim and Victor R. Gold, eds., *Episcopacy in the Lutheran Church: Studies in the Development and Definition of the Office of Church Leadership*, (Fortress Press: Philadelphia, 1970) p. 16.

† Irenaeus of Lyons, *Against Heresies*, Book 3, Chapter 3, Paragraph 3, in the Ante-Nicene Fathers, vol. 1, Eerdmans Publishing Company, Grand Rapids.

wrote this. The dates here are significant. Ignatius, Irenaeus, Tertullian, and others are writing in the 100's and the Apostle John very possibly lived to around A.D. 100. These men were in very close proximity to the apostles themselves. It would be very hard to believe that all of them would have gone so far wrong. "Nowhere is there evidence of a violent struggle such as would be natural if a divinely ordained congregationalism or presbyterianism were overthrown. The same [episcopal] threefold ministry is seen as universal throughout the early church as soon as there is sufficient evidence to show us the nature of the ministry. The conclusion is drawn that episcopacy is the primitive and rightful form of church government."* Now, while we, as Lutherans, would not say that episcopal polity is commanded in the New Testament, episcopacy's very early and nearly universal appearance in the life of the Church lends weight to a reading of the New Testament through episcopal lenses. Perhaps not an episcopacy in its fully-developed form, but the New Testament certainly can be seen to display for us a primitive episcopacy.

From the earliest times to the Reformation, episcopacy is practically the only church polity known in the East or the West: It has a fifteen-hundred-year, universal precedent. That fact, in and of itself, should cause us to seriously think about why we would reject such a massive historical witness and tradition. Not that we need to adopt many of the false notions about the office of bishop that developed early in the Church's life (for example, apostolic succession), but the simple structure of an episcopacy—the office of bishop by human right—has overwhelming support since the very beginning of the Church.

And if that is not enough, many Lutheran churches in the sixteenth century maintained and continued the episcopal

---

* Walter A. Elwell, ed., *Evangelical Dictionary of Theology*, (Baker Book House: Grand Rapids, 1984) p. 239.

polity they inherited from the Roman Catholic Church. Sweden (along with Finland) maintained and continued episcopal polity and do so to this day. This was not a compromise with heresy by those countries, but the normal unfolding of the "conservative Reformation." Even the German lands within the Holy Roman Empire had a few bishops who came over from the old Catholic Church.* In those cases, they did not give up their positions but simply became Lutheran bishops. The "Superintendents" that replaced the Roman Catholic bishops in various German territories carried out the duties of a bishop in many aspects—that is, an evangelical bishop after the precepts laid out in the confessions. If one looks past both the unfortunate disaster of "emergency bishops" in Germany (that is, secular rulers functioning as bishops) and the congregationalist-like experiments of America, one can find many examples of Lutheran episcopal polity throughout history. And the existence of episcopal polity for Lutherans around the world is even more true today than it was at the time of the Reformation. In Germany today, the Lutheran Churches in most of the various states are headed by bishops. They had always in the past been headed by superintendents who were functionally bishops, and now they are called bishops once again. "The superintendents, while in many cases not holding the title of bishop until after World War II, certainly carried out the function of this office, although usually on a more limited geographical scale."† And the problem of "emergency bishops" in Germany is gone now. The idea of the secular ruler being the head of the Church came to an end with the end of the monarchy in 1918. And the various German states adopted the title "bishop" for their ecclesiastical leaders after the world wars—some after the first, the rest after the second. The title "bishop" or "archbishop" is now

* For example: Georg von Polentz, Bishop of Samland 1524–1550; Erhard von Queiss, Bishop of Pomesanien, 1525–1528.

† J.A.O. Preus, *The Second Martin: The Life and Theology of Martin Chemnitz*, Concordia Publishing House, St. Louis, 1994., p. 152.

used once more in all the Scandinavian lands as well.

Even in America today, most Lutherans have a type of episcopal polity. Of course, by saying that, one means that the ELCA has a type of episcopal polity. I'm not saying that the ELCA's episcopacy, or even that of the German Church should be a model for us in all aspects. "Real episcopal authority was diluted by the ELCA's giving quotas confessional standing in choosing its bureaucracy."* But it should be remembered that the title "bishop" was used long before the ELCA was formed: The ALC began using the term in 1970; The LCA and the AELC started using the term in 1980.† The ELCA was founded in 1988 with episcopal polity and the term "bishop." Though there may be aspects of the ELCA's episcopacy that are not appealing, the simple concept of episcopacy, and the term "bishop" are not discredited.

THE CATHOLICITY OF LUTHERANISM AND POLITY

The monk, Vincent of Lérins, in arguing against Augustine's teachings on grace and predestination said, "in the catholic church itself, all possible care should be taken that we hold that which has been believed everywhere, always, and by all (*quod ubique, quod semper, quod ab omnibus*)"‡ Now perhaps we would not want to apply this principle in the way Vincent did against Augustine, and Rome certainly would like to make much out of this position by Vincent, but as a general "rule of thumb," it is not a bad definition (or partial definition) of the term "Catholic." The Lutheran reform-

* *Evangelical and Catholic - A Slogan in Search of a Definition*, David P. Scaer, Paper delivered at the Symposium on the Lutheran Confessions, Fort Wayne, IN, January, 21, 1997, p. 14.

† *The Bishop's Office in the Lutheran Church*, James L. Schaaf, *Trinity Seminary Review*, Fall 1980, vol. 2, no. 2, pp. 9–20.

‡ Quoted in Williston Walker, *A History of the Christian Church*, fourth edition, (Charles Scribner's Sons: New York, 1985), p. 210.

ers upheld this notion of catholicity when they concluded the Augsburg Confession with these words, "...we have related only matters which we have considered it necessary to adduce and mention in order that it may be made very clear that we have introduced nothing, either in doctrine or in ceremonies, that is contrary to Holy Scripture or the universal Christian Church."* The English of the *Concordia Triglotta* and the Jacobs edition of the *Book of Concord*, both follow the Latin and use "Catholic" rather than "universal" here. Nevertheless, the meaning is the same. The Lutheran Church is by definition a Catholic Church. Again the Augsburg Confession says, "Inasmuch as our churches dissent from the church catholic in no article of faith but only omit some few abuses which are new and have been adopted by the fault of the times..."† All three creeds proclaim us to be Catholics in spite of modern prejudice against the term. All three creeds proclaim us to be Catholics in spite of the obsolete and thoroughly confusing use of a fifteenth century German idiom in our modern English hymnals, that is, the word "Christian" substituted for the original "Catholic" (*The Lutheran Hymnal* and *Lutheran Worship*). The term "Christian" in the creeds is, in our modern context, thoroughly misleading. It, in fact, obscures the truth and creates misunderstanding among the laity.

The concept of catholicity is indispensable to Lutheran theology. It is necessary to believe that the Holy Spirit works in and through creation. That He has been working through the Church in the history of the world. Sometimes in larger, and sometimes in smaller streams, the true Church of Christ has remained and continues to live. Sometimes there has only been a small remnant, but the true Church has always existed in history. This is a particular view of salvation

---

* Theodore G. Tappert, ed., *The Book of Concord* (Fortress Press: Philadelphia, 1959), p. 95.

† Tappert, p. 48. Latin text.

history: one of continuity. If this continuity is not true, then one must wonder whether Christ's words about the gates of hell not prevailing over the Church are true? If there is no living continuity in the Church, how shall we know where the true Church is? Shall we begin to look for miraculous signs to identify the Church, to see where it has popped up in *this* generation? If the Holy Spirit abandons creation for certain periods of time—that is, the world is without the true Church—then can we be sure that He is working for our salvation today? Can we be sure He works in the water of Baptism, or the elements of the Eucharist? Has the Holy Spirit tied Himself to this world—and to the tangible elements of this world—or not? Or can we never be sure if the Church exists, or where grace can be found? Perhaps the Jehovah's Witness's are right about history, or the Gnostics are, or the Arians? But, no, God *does* inhabit His Church. There is a living tradition in the Church that does not contradict the Gospel. We should remain in the broad stream of the church catholic as much as is possible.

Even if the Church is but a remnant, the Church must continue the teaching of Christ and the apostles until Christ's return. Continuity with all ages of the Church is vital to the stability of the faith and to the strengthening of the doctrines of the Incarnation, the Sacraments, the Church, and office of the ministry. If Lutherans are just a bunch of discontented, drunken Germans and Swedes turned into a denomination, then there is no valid reason for its existence. If we can't claim continuity with the apostles, then are we teaching new doctrines, practicing new ceremonies? The Book of Concord answers the question clearly: It proclaims the Lutheran Church to be the continuing Catholic Church in its purity, and Rome a distorted and error ridden caricature of Catholicism. But Lutherans have long since forgotten this perspective. While Rome fatally diverged from apostolic and catholic teaching in many ways (especially regarding Justification), it has maintained much that is Catholic in its worship and piety and polity. Lutherans, meanwhile, have used the idea of *adiaphora* (things neither commanded nor forbidden in Scripture) to avoid all things Catholic. In popular thinking, being Lutheran is to be anti-Catholic. I would argue that if one does not see one's self as a Catholic, consciously, then one is not a Lutheran. One may be a generic Protestant, an anti-Roman Catholic, but not a Lutheran. Our creeds and our confessions demand that we be conscious Catholics. And by that standard, how many Lutherans are there in the world?

AN EVANGELICAL BISHOP

In Germany, "The chief function of the superintendent was the supervision of the doctrine and life of the pastors, their education and examination, and the overall care of the congregations."* Luther himself gives guidance in his *Instructions for the Visitors of Parish Pastors in Electoral Saxony* (1528), where he says:

> This pastor (*Pfarrherr*) shall be superintendent of all the other priests who have their parish or benefice in the region, whether they live in monasteries or foundations of nobles or of others. He shall make sure that in these parishes there is correct Christian teaching, that the Word of God and the holy Gospel are truly and purely proclaimed, and that the holy Sacraments according to the institution of Christ are provided to the blessing of the people. The preachers are to exemplify a good life so that the people take no offence but better their own lives. They are not to teach or preach anything that is contrary to the Word of God or that contributes to rebellion against the government. If one or more of the pastors or preachers is

* *The Second Martin.*, p. 152.

> guilty of error in this or that respect, the superintendent shall call to himself those concerned and have them abstain from it, but also carefully instruct them wherein they are guilty and have erred either in commission or omission, either in doctrine or in life."[*]

The Lutheran Confessions, however, don't say a great deal about episcopal polity because its existence was not a matter of dispute. The office of oversight was a normal part of the Church. What is addressed in the confessions are the abuses in which the contemporary Roman bishops were engaged. From certain responses to abuses found in the confessions, we can get some ideas as to what an Evangelical Lutheran bishop looks like. Augsburg Confession article 28 clearly teaches that ecclesiastical authority and civil authority ought to be clearly distinguished. It also teaches that bishops, like all clergy, have the power of the keys, that is, the power "to preach the Gospel, to forgive and retain sins, and to administer and distribute the Sacraments."[†] And again, article 28 says, "According to divine right, therefore, it is the office of the bishop to preach the Gospel, forgive sins, judge doctrine and condemn doctrine that is contrary to the Gospel, and exclude from the Christian community the ungodly whose wicked conduct is manifest."[‡] Once again, this is no different from parish pastors—bishops are part of the one office of the ministry, but by human arrangement they supervise other clergy. However, note the power that is given to all clergy—parish pastors or bishops—in article 28: the authority to excommunicate. Contrary to some popular opinions, it is not a power given to the voter's assembly. The Apology says, "We like the old division of power into the power of the order and the power of jurisdiction. Therefore

---

* Quoted in J.A.O. Preus, *The Second Martin*, Luther's Works, American Edition, vol. 40, p. 313.

† Tappert, *The Book of Concord*, p. 81. Article 28 "The Power of Bishops"

‡ Ibid., p. 84.

a bishop has the power of the order, namely, the ministry of Word and Sacraments. He also has the power of jurisdiction, namely, the authority to excommunicate those who are guilty of public offenses or to absolve them if they are converted and ask for absolution."'* And the *Augustana* acknowledges that this power is by divine right, "On this account parish ministers [*Pfarrleute*] and churches are bound to be obedient to the bishops according to the saying of Christ in Luke 10:16, "He who hears you hears me."'† Those who would oppose this sort of clerical authority might cite Matthew 18:17 as giving power of excommunication to the voters, "If he [your brother] refuses to listen to them [one or two other brothers], tell it to the church; and if he refuses to listen even to the church, treat him as you would a pagan or a tax collector." Anti-clerical Lutherans assume that the congregation (presumably in a voter's assembly) retains the authority to exercise the keys. But the passage does not teach any such thing. The pastor still exercises the keys for the congregation. And as Lutherans, we acknowledge that it is only those who are regularly called who exercise the keys as officers of the church.

I am not advocating for an all powerful clergy. An Evangelical bishop does not have arbitrary power. Over and over again in the Confessions, it is stated that a bishop is to be disobeyed if he institutes or commands anything that is "contrary" to the Gospel. This supreme loyalty to the Word of God prevents an Evangelical bishop from having as much power as a Roman bishop, but also prevents corrupting power to a certain extent. The institutional church can never be the ultimate loyalty for an Evangelical bishop.

The word "contrary" in the confessions is important, in that warnings in the confessions against unscriptural bish-

---

* Tappert, *The Book of Concord*, Apology, article 28, p. 238.

† Tappert, *The Book of Concord*, Augsburg Confession, article 28, p. 84.

ops do not mean that bishops must be bound only to specific commands in scripture, the warnings are against bishops who teach "contrary" to the scriptures. Bishops still have authority in *adiaphora*. Article 28 of the *Augustana* says, "What are we to say, then, about Sunday and other similar church ordinances and ceremonies? To this our teachers reply that bishops or pastors may make regulations so that everything in the churches is done in good order, ... It is proper for the Christian assembly to keep such ordinances for the sake of love and peace, to be obedient to the bishops and parish ministers [*Pfarrherren*] in such matters,"* As we can see, the Confessions don't give any specific powers by divine right to bishops. Bishops and parish pastors have by divine right the same office. A church simply agrees to give a supervisory role to some pastors. The Smalcald Articles concede ordination and confirmation to bishops out of tradition, but not of necessity.†

THE MOTIVATING ISSUES

What's the real problem that brings this issue of episcopacy before us, for our consideration? What difference does polity or even nomenclature make? For example, Missouri Synod district presidents already function as bishops in some ways. They do oversee the placement of pastors in congregations, they even make the placements themselves for candidates directly out of seminary. They do oversee ordinations, and often ordain candidates themselves. Theoretically, they are supposed to oversee the spiritual life of the congregations in their district, although it is hard to see how that is possible given the size of the current LCMS districts. This situation applies to ELCA bishops as well. The real issue, the unacceptable situation, is the utter lack of clerical

* Ibid., p. 89–90.

† Tappert, *The Book of Concord*, Smalcald Articles, Part 3, Article 10. p. 314.

authority in the typical Lutheran congregation. Pastors who are honest will admit this is a real problem. Parish pastors are essentially hired employees of the congregation. This situation is found in all the current American Lutheran church bodies beyond our diocese. All the protestation from certain scholars and pastors that this anti-clericalism is not really the Missouri Synod historical model is useless, it is still the fact in real life. In far too many circumstances, the parish pastor cannot be a spiritual father to his flock, because he cannot give them medicine they need, but don't want. Congregational autonomy from the district and the synod, even the pay structure for clergy, has a devastating impact on the ability of the pastor to do his job effectively. Pastors cannot be helped by district presidents in the LCMS whose positions are advisory, and a pastor is too beholden to the sensibilities of the congregation which might cut off his salary at any time. Though many congregations would not do this, there are sadly too many that would. Pastors are constantly told that catechesis is the answer. Education is held up as the key to success and happiness, as if the only problem is a lack of knowledge in the Church. It is implied that once the people know what is correct they will choose it. It seems as if we have abolished the concept of sin. The word "catechesis" is spoken of as if it were an almost magical word. But, if all the pastor has is catechesis, he can always be dismissed as a "flake." "That's just your opinion, pastor" is what will be heard from many corners. In the current Missouri Synod system of polity, the parish pastor is on his own. The district president is merely advisory. The real issue is pastoral authority, not the ability to tyrannize, but the ability to do what is right even if it is unpopular. Is a local congregation under the authority of their parish pastor and their bishop, or are they an autonomous voter's assembly? Given the current system in the Missouri Synod, a parish pastor far too often must either give the people what they want, or become a master manipulator. Neither are desirable characteristics for a pastor. What virtue is there in a polity which forces a pastor to fight for his clerical life because he wants to institute weekly communion? Such a pastor must have an authoritative bishop behind him. I am not arguing here for the ability to tyrannize the laity. I am simply arguing for the ability to be a real shepherd, a real spiritual father—to do the right thing by the sheep even when they don't like it. Any father would do what was best for his children even when they complained about it. Think of the absurdity of it: if a father had to rely on simple catechesis to get his children not to stay up until midnight, or eat candy for breakfast, lunch, and dinner.

Anti-authoritarianism is a particular problem for Americans. Americans are used to voting for, or choosing, everything. They've grown up with that world view—It is in the air they breath, and the water they drink. And Americans have an amazingly naive confidence in their own ability to perceive reality clearly and make the right decisions. They are used to being in control, controlling their futures, their finances, the natural world around them, and especially their choices with regard to consumer goods. One might say Americans are consumers. And this consumer mentality unconsciously extends even to God Himself. Many Americans construct their god out of their consumer preferences. They will not accept anything undesirable in their god. They want God to be the way they expect Him to be. They want Him to be in line with their sensibilities. Americans don't want a sovereign God any more than they want a sovereign king. And they don't want a Church that makes them conform their consumer preferences to something outside of themselves, an objective standard. But this is precisely what the American consumer needs. He needs one place that does not bow to his will, one place where the customer isn't always right. One place where he can learn obedience to a higher will, to knock down the self and conform the self to Christ. Episcopacy helps in learning that lesson. It helps to remind us that not everything is in our power, in our control. We cannot choose everything in our lives. Thomas à Kempis wrote beautifully concerning obedience:

> It is a very great thing to obey, to live under a superior and not to be one's own master, for it is much safer to be subject than it is to command. Many live in obedience more from necessity than from love. Such become discontented and dejected on the slightest pretext; they will never gain peace of mind unless they subject themselves whole-heartedly for the love of God. Go where you may, you will find no rest except in humble obedience to the rule of authority. Dreams of happiness expected from change and different places have deceived many.*

I find obedience and subjection as hard as the next man. I don't claim to have perfected it, but an episcopal polity in the Church more readily helps us learn those virtues. They are virtues sorely needed in our Church.

THE CULTURE OF PIETY: BEING CHURCHLY

And beyond the structure, the nuts and bolts of episcopacy, we should want the traditional trappings, the packaging of episcopacy. Why should we use terms like "bishop" and "archbishop?" Because these are recognized "churchly" terms. Everyone knows that a "bishop" is the head of a Church. "President" is not specifically churchly, for example, news paper reporters, when reporting about the Missouri Synod, have to explain to their readers what "president" means. They say things like "president, that is, what

* Thomas à Kempis, *The Imitation of Christ*, The Bruce Publishing Company, Milwaukee, 1940., p. 12.

other churches would call bishops." The term "bishop" is churchly and recognizable, "presidents" are heads of governments or corporations or civic clubs. If we want to cultivate a churchly or pious environment, then we ought to start talking like churchmen rather than corporate executives. One of the greatest problems we face in the Church today is the secularization of the minds and hearts of Christians. When the Church looks and sounds and acts more like the secular world, things will go very badly. We need to create and nurture a churchly, an otherworldly environment within the Church. We need bishops and archbishops with miters and croziers. We need leaders who look and speak and think in "other-worldly" ways. Bishops who are unashamedly ecclesial, not self conscious about wearing this or that, or fearful that they might look too "stuffy." Being overtly and consciously churchly is not a vice. It is comforting and assuring. Anglican and Roman bishops are not hypocrites because they look and act the part. They are doing their jobs. On one level we are all hypocrites and pretend to be more than we are. Even the Amish can turn plainness into pride. We need bishops who are experts in doctrine, prayer, and worship. Perhaps if we had bishops, we too might look and sound a bit more sacred, a bit more churchly. And perhaps, if we as a Church looked the part and sounded the part, we might start to act the part as well.

One can always hear the protests from the expected sources whenever anyone advocates episcopacy. "If you establish bishops, they will start acting like bishops." Presumably "acting like a bishop" is a bad thing. There is a great fear of episcopal authority. Could men with episcopal powers eventually corrupt and pervert an orthodox church body? Yes. Is it almost an inevitability? If history is any indicator, yes. It does seem as if every church body in the history of the world has run its course from original purity to organizational corruption. But episcopacy will not do that any faster than any other form of government. It seems as if there is an unspoken assumption within the Missouri Synod, that decentralized polity is the magic formula that will keep any church organization sound and healthy. The assumption is, liberal and unfaithful clergy will lead us down the path to ruin, but highly democratic forms of government will preserve us safe and sound. We seem to have very little confidence in our clergy (rightly or wrongly), and a lot of confidence in democracy. That can't bode well for the Church.

APOSTOLIC SUCCESSION

The subject of apostolic succession is not strictly part of what is being considered in this paper, but it is so often a topic with regard to episcopacy that I would like to make a brief mention of it. Should Lutherans care about so called apostolic succession? For the most part, the answer should be no. Lutherans have no problem obtaining or maintaining "apostolic succession" for the sake of tradition or for the sake of a weaker brother's conscience. However, Lutherans ought not be in the business of obtaining "apostolic succession" in order to make some other group or organization see them as legitimate. Chasing after Roman or Eastern or Anglican approval through "apostolic succession" plays into the doctrinal errors of these churches. They make lists of successive office holders the test as to their own orthodoxy, rather than an examination of doctrine that is passed on. If Roman apostolic succession can't keep Popes from kissing Korans or praying with imams in mosques, I fail to see its value. Likewise, Anglican apostolic succession hasn't stopped the Archbishop of Canterbury from being an honorary Druid. (I still like Hermann Sasse's treatment of the subject thus far in the *We Confess Anthology*.)*

* Hermann Sasse, *We Confess Anthology*, (Concordia Publishing House, Saint Louis, 1999).

We should also note that there is no sort of "apostolic succession" that Lutherans can obtain that will make Rome or the East view their orders as valid. A Lutheran Church body's "Lutheranism" invalidates any succession. Neither Rome nor the East recognize the Swedish succession, which is probably the only one worth having for a Lutheran in regard to tradition.

The Church of Sweden has had apostolic succession since Stefan was consecrated Archbishop of Uppsala in A.D. 1164 by Pope Alexander III and the Archbishop of Lund, who was made Primate over Uppsala. Uppsala became independent of Lund when Folke Johansson Ängel was consecrated as Archbishop of Uppsala directly by Pope Gregory X in A.D. 1274. During the Reformation, Laurentius Petri was elected Archbishop of Uppsala by all the pastors of Sweden. "The Consecration took place on 22nd September 1531 at Stockholm, being performed by Petrus Magni, Bishop of Västeras, who had himself been confirmed and consecrated by the authority of Pope Clement VII in 1524."[*] "It was through this bishop that the Apostolic Succession was preserved in the Church of Sweden."[†]

This succession has been passed to others. The Church of Finland and all three Baltic Lutheran Churches also have their apostolic succession through Sweden. But, once again, neither the East nor Rome recognize this succession. Only the Anglicans are impressed with the Swedish pedigree. If the ELDoNA were to have this Swedish succession made available to her, it might be worth getting so long as she would not have to compromise herself in any way. The Swedish apostolic succession might be a nice bit of historic, traditional "window dressing," but certainly nothing essential.

---

* Eric E. Yelverton, *An Archbishop of the Reformation*, (The Epworth Press, London, 1958) p. 5.

† Ibid., p. 5 note.

CONCLUSION

"More Christians accept episcopacy than any other form of church government."* Episcopacy is the historic polity of the Church, and the most widely accepted polity around the world. It is Catholic. And this is perhaps the greatest argument for the adoption of episcopacy. It is the Catholic thing to do. And as Catholics it should be the thing we want to do. Are we Catholics as we confess each Sunday in our creeds? It seems that the decisive factor in the hearts and minds of individual Lutherans is: How seriously they take their creedal confession of being Catholic. Does one really wish to be Catholic? Does one really wish to embrace, as much as is possible, the entire history of the Church? Does one really wish to be, as much as is theologically possible, in harmony with the Church around the world today? Of course, we must reject the errors of Rome, but since we are Catholics, shouldn't we wish to reject only that which we absolutely have to? If one really takes being a Catholic seriously, then episcopacy seems to be impossible to reject. Any episcopacy that a Lutheran adopts must be a true, Evangelical episcopacy, but an episcopacy nonetheless. We perhaps need to ask ourselves what our real identity is? What is the principle that forms our identity? Is it being an American, being a "Protestant," or being a Catholic? If one sees oneself as an Evangelical Catholic, there seems to be no choice but to embrace episcopacy.

What are the most important reasons for adopting episcopal polity?

1) It is the Catholic thing to do. If we are truly Catholic then

---

* Walter A. Elwell, ed., *Evangelical Dictionary of Theology*, p. 239.

we will not ignore or reject something that the Church Catholic has done practically for its entire existence. Can one even truly be a Lutheran and not a Catholic?

2) It is the confessional thing to do. The Lutheran Confessions do not demand episcopal polity, but they do assume it, and the confessors express there "earnest desire," and "deep desire to maintain the church polity and various ranks of the ecclesiastical hierarchy." This clear preference of the confessors of Augsburg ought to have the greatest weight upon the issue of episcopal polity.

3) The New Testament seems to imply a primitive episcopal polity, at least in the Greek world in which St. Paul worked. The New Testament commands no particular form of church polity, but it does give legitimacy to the form that soon became the norm in the Church.

4) There is a great need among Christians to learn the virtues of obedience to authority generally, and clerical authority in particular. In a culture dominated by liberty and independence, submission is not an easy virtue to develop, but it is absolutely essential for a healthy church.

5) An episcopacy, with all the trappings that go with it, is a more recognizably sacred arrangement to the world at large. If we are going to be "churchly," we need to look and sound the part.

The Evangelical Lutheran Diocese of North America is not perfectly structured or organized. We have existed now, for just over a year. We are trying, to the best of our ability, to construct an episcopally structured Lutheran church body. We pray that our efforts will glorify our Lord, Jesus Christ, and serve as a starting point for the rebuilding of the Lutheran Church on this continent.

Episcopal Polity in Historic Lutheranism*

My intention with this paper is to make a reasonable defense of episcopal polity in the Lutheran Church from a doctrinal and historical standpoint. I do not intend to convince everyone of the value and merit of episcopal polity. Some people will disagree no matter what I say and that is, of course, their prerogative. I wish them God's blessings as they try to be faithful to their calling in Christ. My modest goal is to show that episcopal polity is highly defensible from our doctrinal sources and from our history. And while I believe it is the preferred polity for the Lutheran Church—and I will argue from that perspective—it is by no means necessary to the existence of the Church. I believe episcopal polity is a very important issue but it is, ultimately, an *adiaphoron*. And I make this point because I realize that in the Synodical Conference culture that most of us have come from, episcopal polity is a little bit of a foreign idea. I know that many may never be comfortable enough with such a polity to join one, but that may not be necessary. The ministerium of the Evangelical Lutheran Diocese of North America is united in its understanding that polity is not divisive of fellowship. Church bodies may be separate organizations and yet have full fellowship with each other. The ELDoNA can easily see itself in fellowship with church bodies that are not episcopally ordered. So, we are here with all of you, at this conference, to explore what fellowship possibilities exist. Let us all

* Presented at the 2008 Winter Confessional Lutheran Free Conference (31 January 2008) in Burnsville, Minnesota.

hope and pray for unity among those of a confessional mind so that our great Confession may continue in this land.

POLITY IN THE LUTHERAN CONFESSIONS

I'll not touch all that much upon the issue of a divinely established office of the ministry; it is likely to lead us too far astray. I assume that all here agree that the office of the ministry is established in the Scriptures, and that our confession of that office is first found in articles five and fourteen of the *Augustana.*

Perhaps fewer here would agree with us in the ELDoNA that "Ordination is not an *adiaphoron.* It is part of a right understanding of a proper call."* We would cite the *Treatise on the Power and Primacy of the Pope* (§65), where it says; "it is manifest that ordination administered by a pastor in his own church is valid by divine right."† But even though we might disagree about some things, I'm sure we can agree in principle to a commitment to the Lutheran Confessions.

So, let us focus more specifically on polity in the Confessions, and see what the Confessions say about episcopacy. In the *Apology of the Augsburg Confession,* Philip Melanchthon (with Luther's approval) expressed a very definite opinion with regard to episcopacy. He said:

---

* Niles Theses, Theses number four. I will quote Dr. David Scaer here: "Luther held ordination as necessary. This opinion was offered in the case of a certain Johann Sutel who had assumed the position of preacher at St. Nicolai Church in Gottingen. Luther was asked the question whether Sutel could celebrate the Eucharist without priestly ordination, priesterliche Weihe. His reply was no. Sutel should refrain from the celebration till he was ordained." *Ordination: Human Rite or Divine Ordinance,* (Concordia Theological Seminary Press, Fort Wayne, 1977).

† *Treatise on the Power and Primacy of the Pope,* § 65. Theodore G. Tappert, ed., *The Book of Concord,* (Fortress Press, Philadelphia) 1959, p. 331. (Jacobs, p. 349; Kolb/Wengert, p. 340.)

> On this matter [church order] we have given frequent testimony in the assembly to our deep desire to maintain the church polity and various ranks of the ecclesiastical hierarchy, although they were created by human authority. ... Thus the cruelty of the bishops is the reason for the abolition of canonical government in some places, despite our earnest desire to keep it. ... Furthermore, we want at this point to declare our willingness to keep the ecclesiastical and canonical polity, provided that the bishops stop raging against our churches. This willingness will be our defense, both before God and among all nations, present and future, against the charge that we have undermined the authority of the bishops.*

When Melanchthon says that the Lutherans desire to keep the polity and hierarchy of the Church, he is referring, of course, to the only polity and hierarchy which existed at that time: the Catholic polity and hierarchy. Melanchthon was, of course, trying to find as much ground for agreement as possible. These were not thoughtless comments on Melanchthon's part. Melanchthon spent a good deal of time considering his response to the Roman theologians of the *Confutation.* It should be remembered that the Roman theologians of the *Confutation of the Augsburg Confession* agreed with article fourteen. They found nothing in the words of the article with which to disagree. They simply inserted their concern for canonical polity, and said they agreed with article fourteen so long as canonical polity was upheld. It should also be remembered that the Lutherans, when considering their reply to the *Confutation*, were denied a copy of it in order to frame their *Apology*. However, Melanchthon remembered very well the objections of the *Confutation* because "for three months he represented the Lutherans on a

---

* *Apology of the Augsburg Confession*, article 14, § 1,2 and 5. Tappert, pp. 214–215. (Jacobs, p. 217; Kolb/Wengert, pp. 222–223.)

large committee appointed by the emperor to consider the possibility of a doctrinal agreement between the two sides.'"* Melanchthon was trying to eliminate any unnecessary divisions between the Lutherans and Rome. In the *Apology* he makes it clear that he has no problem with canonical polity itself (in fact, he wants to maintain it), but complains that the Roman authorities are making it impossible. Melanchthon holds out an olive branch to the Roman theologians, in essence saying, "polity need not divide us unless you make it divisive." This is Melanchthon's response to Roman hierarchy, and it was not something that Melanchthon slipped past his colleagues, or the princes, or Luther. They would not have approved had Melanchthon given up some essential doctrine in the *Apology.* So, it might come as a shock to Lutherans today that it was Luther's and Melanchthon's "deep desire," and "earnest desire" (to quote the *Apology*) to keep the hierarchy and polity of episcopacy, but it is quite clearly what they confessed. And this desire of the Lutheran confessors was not something that was limited or conditioned to the sixteenth century. Melanchthon says that this "deep desire"—this "willingness"—would be their defense against charges of an anti-episcopal attitude for both the "present and future."

Now, it seems to me that this article in the *Apology* is overwhelming evidence that polity is an *adiaphoron* for Lutherans. Luther and Melanchthon have no problem maintaining Roman canonical polity for the sake of the Gospel. And if this article is not clear enough on that subject, let us remember how Philip subscribed to the *Smalcald Articles*, "...concerning the pope I hold that, if he would allow the Gospel, we, too, may concede to him that superiority over the bishops which he possesses by human right, making this concession for the sake of peace and general unity among

* J.L. Neve, *Story and Significance of The Augsburg Confession*, (The Lutheran Literary Board, Burlington, Iowa, 1930) p. 76.

Christians who are now under him and may be in the future.'"[*] Lutherans certainly did not make an issue out of polity.

Now, beyond the fact that polity is an *adiaphoron*, article fourteen of the *Apology* gives us a good argument for preferring episcopal polity to other polities. Once again, to be clear, article fourteen makes no law requiring episcopal polity—but does not the "deep desire" and the "earnest desire" of the writer of the *Apology* carry significant weight when determining our desires on the subject? Not only was this the private desire of Melanchthon or Luther (and it was), but it is also the "deep desire" expressed as part of the Church's symbols. These phrases could have been removed before subscription if they caused discomfort to the Lutheran fathers. They were not removed. Of course, as events progressed in the German lands, a continuation of the then-current episcopacy proved impossible. The vast majority of the existing German bishops remained in communion with the pope.[†] But the necessary changes in practice among the German Lutherans did not negate the principle expressed in article fourteen of the *Apology*—that it was still their "deep desire to maintain the church polity and various ranks of the ecclesiastical hierarchy."

Not only do the Lutheran Confessors see episcopal polity as and *adiaphoron*, and as their preferred polity, they also simply assume it to be the norm for the Church. In article 28 of the *Augsburg Confession* the term "bishops"[‡] is used in addition to parish pastors. The main issue addressed in article 28 was the problem of the confusion of the spiritual and

* Smalcald Articles, part III, signatures. Tappert, pp. 316–317. (Jacobs, pp. 336-337; Kolb/Wengert, p. 326.)

† There were a small number of bishops in the German lands who did become Lutheran bishops. For example: Georg von Polentz, Bishop of Samland (1524–1550) and Erhard von Queiss, Bishop of Pomesanien (1525–1528).

‡ *Bischöfe*; *episcoporum*.

secular realms; that is, the power appropriate to the Church and the power appropriate to the State. Medieval Christendom had practically no distinctions between the two realms: bishops and archbishops were at the same time the rulers of various territories. The Lutherans were clearly complaining about that abuse. Also, they complained generally of bishops making human traditions binding on consciences. But the Lutheran confessors did not simply denounce bishops for being bishops. They only complained about the abuses. In fact, the Lutheran confessors gave guidelines for what a true evangelical bishop should be:

> According to divine right, therefore, it is the office of the bishop [*episcopis*] to preach the Gospel, forgive sins, judge doctrine and condemn doctrine that is contrary to the Gospel, and exclude from the Christian community the ungodly whose wicked conduct is manifest. All this is to be done not by human power but by God's Word alone. On this account parish ministers [*Pfarrleute*] and churches [*Kirchen*] are bound to be obedient to the bishops [*Bischöfen*] according to the saying of Christ in Luke 10:16, "He who hears you hears me."*

Note that what is talked about in the quotation above specifically applies to bishops in distinction from "parish ministers and churches." Granted, what applies here to bishops applies to all in the office of the ministry, since there is only one divinely-instituted office. Nevertheless, Melanchthon uses the term "bishop" here in distinction from a parish pastor. Article 28 lists other points of authority a bishop has:

> What are we to say, then, about Sunday and other similar church ordinances and ceremonies? To this our teachers reply that bishops [*Bischöfe*] or pastors

* Augsburg Confession, article 28, § 21–22, German text. Tappert, p. 84. (Jacobs, p. 62. Kolb/Wengert, p. 94.)

> [*Pfarrherren*] may make regulations so that everything in the churches is done in good order, ... It is proper for the Christian assembly to keep such ordinances for the sake of love and peace, to be obedient to bishops [*Bischöfe*] and parish ministers [*Pfarrherren*] in such matters.*

Once again, the three-fold distinction within the one office of the ministry is assumed as normal to the Lutheran reformers. Luther himself makes the distinction in the Table of Duties of the Small Catechism. He entitled the first duty; "*Den Bischöfen, Pfarrherren und Predigern.*" "For Bishops, Pastors, and Preachers."† Yes, what is taught in this first duty applies to everyone in the office of the ministry, but Luther has in mind the historical three-fold division of the one office.

Luther also acknowledges that there can be such a thing as a "true bishop" in the Lutheran Church. In the *Smalcald Articles*, Luther severely criticizes the then-current bishops in Germany. He says:

> If bishops [*Bischöfe/episcopi*] were true bishops and were concerned about the church and the Gospel, they might be permitted (for the sake of love and unity, but not of necessity) to ordain and confirm us and our preachers, provided this could be done without pretense, humbug, and unchristian ostentation. However, they neither are nor wish to be true bishops.‡

With all of Luther's very valid criticism, he acknowledges the theoretical possibility of "true bishops" in the Lu-

* *Augsburg Confession*, article 28, § 53 and 55, German text. Tappert, pp. 89–90. (Jacobs, p. 65. Kolb/Wengert, p. 98.)

† *Small Catechism*, [IX] Table of Duties, § 2, Tappert, p. 354. (Jacobs, p. 376. Kolb/Wengert, p. 365.)

‡ *Smalcald Articles*, part III, article X, § 1. Tappert, pp. 314. (Jacobs, pp. 333–334; Kolb/Wengert, p. 323–324.)

theran Church. He doesn't want to eliminate bishops; he simply wants them to be evangelical bishops.

Even passages that have been used by some against episcopal polity are not at all against episcopal polity, but against papal claims of supremacy over the other bishops, or they were against the Roman bishops and Pope cutting off their possibilities for pastors in the future. Rome would try to deprive the Lutherans of bishops. In such a case, the essential truth that the keys belong to the Church was defended. The confessions do not argue against bishops as such, they argue against the corruption of the bishops.

LUTHERAN EPISCOPACY IN HISTORY

SWEDEN

At the outset of the Reformation, the Lutheran confessors were eager to maintain the historic episcopacy. There is nothing in Lutheran doctrine that militates against episcopacy. The loss of Episcopal polity in some places was forced upon the Lutherans because of the hostility of the Roman Church. Sweden is the country most often talked about when speaking of Lutheran episcopacy because the Church of Sweden, in fact, maintained much of the pre-Reformation polity it had received. In the early 1520's when King Gustavus Vasa ascended to power, he was inclined to settle scores with the bishops who sided with his enemy, Denmark. He often replaced Romanist-sympathizing bishops with Evangelical bishops when vacancies occurred (sometimes vacancies occurred because the former bishops fled the country). This was the case with Laurentius Petri Nericius, who was named the new archbishop of Uppsala in 1531.

When Gustavus Vasa assumed the Swedish throne in

> 1523, five sees stood vacant. He sought to fill these in approved canonical fashion and succeeded in the case of Petrus Magni, who was consecrated with papal approval in Rome in 1524. In 1528 Petrus Magni consecrated three bishops, and in 1531 Laurentius Petri was consecrated archbishop (possibly by Petrus Magni).*

Dr. Eric Yelverton says more confidently: "The Consecration took place on 22nd September 1531 at Stockholm, being performed by Petrus Magni, Bishop of Västeras, who had himself been confirmed and consecrated by the authority of Pope Clement VII in 1524."† And Tighe writes:

> Laurentius Petri was a young priest and schoolmaster who had received his theological education at Wittenberg in Luther's early reforming years. In his liturgical reforms in Sweden from the 1540s onward he was to show himself one of the most conservative of Reformers, but on other matters he was thoroughly Lutheran, believing (as he was to state in his preface to the Church Order of 1571) that while bishops fulfilled a necessary function in the Church of oversight and discipline, and would therefore no doubt remain until the end of the world, there was nevertheless only one ordained office in the church, the "*Predikoambetet*," or preaching office, or priesthood, and that bishops were simply priests to whom certain necessary supervisory functions had been assigned."‡

---

* *Episcopacy: Lutheran-United Methodist Dialogue II*, Jack M. Tuell and Roger W. Fjeld, editors., (Augsburg Fortress: Minneapolis, 1991) p. 49.

† Eric E. Yelverton, *An Archbishop of the Reformation*, (The Epworth Press: London, 1958) p. 5.

‡ William Tighe, *The Swedish Episcopal Succession, http://reader.classicalanglican.net/?page_id=315*

It seems that for roughly the first fifteen years of the Reformation in Sweden, King Gustavus Vasa was interested in maintaining the old hierarchical order. However, "Beginning in 1540 King Gustav seems to have decided to abolish the episcopate, and as bishops died… men termed *Ordinarii* (or later Superintendents) were appointed in their places."* It looked as if Sweden was going to follow the lead of Germany and Denmark in abolishing the historic episcopate in their countries. So, it seems that there were two opposite realities in Sweden after 1540: the remnants of an historic episcopal polity, and strong anti-episcopal pressure from the crown—at least until the reign of King Johan III.

> During this transitional period it seems that the consecrations of Michael Agricola and Paulus Juusten for sees in Finland by Botvid Sunesson of Strängnäs were regarded as valid episcopal consecrations. Some continuity was restored in Sweden with the appointment of Laurentius Petri Gotha as archbishop in 1575. Among the participants in the consecration was Juusten. Scholarly opinion is divided over whether an episcopal *successio personalis* survived in the Swedish church during this period. But it is certain that the prevailing Lutheran pattern eventually established itself in Sweden. For the most part the term "bishop" was discarded, superintendents were charged with duties of oversight, and pastors as well as bishops conducted ordinations. That these things are not reflected in the present episcopal regime in the Church of Sweden is the result of developments in the nineteenth century. Throughout Scandinavia the episcopal office was dramatically reformed. The office of oversight was regarded as an ecclesiastical convention rather than a divine invention. In the generations following the reform, the Scandina-

* Ibid.

> vians generally called their ordinaries "superintendent" (*superintendent* or *superattendent*) rather than "bishop." They did not return to the older usage for generations. Although forms of cooperation with the civil authorities differed in the various states, duties of oversight in the Scandinavian churches were prescribed much as in Germany.*

We should not romanticize the Lutheran episcopacy in Sweden. While the historic episcopacy was intentionally preserved in the early years of the Reformation, and then by the crown towards the end of the sixteenth century, it was not such an important part of the life of the Church in Sweden. In the nineteenth century (probably contemporaneously with England's Oxford Movement) some in Sweden began to reemphasize historic nomenclature and the so-called "apostolic succession." Now, there is nothing wrong with reclaiming traditions and historic practices (in fact, I would argue strongly for doing just that). But for a very long time, the Swedish Reformation strongly reflected the Reformation in Germany, except for the technical retention of the episcopacy. There was no real difference in how they viewed the office of oversight in the Church. The offices held by Martin Chemnitz and Laurentius Petri Nericius were the same thing in essence, but had different forms of consecration and different titles. Still, they were both functionally Evangelical bishops.

Laurentius Petri Nericius died in 1573. The consecration of the next archbishop of Uppsala—Laurentius Petri Gothus—took place on July 14, 1575. This consecration was performed by four "bishops"—however, it is clear that three of the four had never been consecrated themselves, including the principal consecrator. The one of the four who had been consecrated was Bishop Paul Juusten of Abo, in

---

* *Episcopacy,* Tuell and Fjeld, pp. 49–50.

Finland. It appears that after the consecration of Laurentius Petri Gothus, consecrations continued in a regular way for the archbishops of Uppsala thereafter.

LATVIA

The Baltic peoples, including the Latvians, were some of the last people in Europe to be converted to Christianity: Christian missionaries did not arrive in the area until around A.D. 1180. Nevertheless, Latvia was in the forefront of embracing the Reformation and this should forever be to their great credit. (Luther even wrote a letter to them in A.D. 1523.) However, the transition from Roman Catholicism to Lutheranism was not a grass-roots movement. The Lutheran Reformation took hold first among the German upper classes. The head of the military-religious order of knights promoted Lutheran teachings for his own political purposes. And the merchants, property owners, and artisans in the city of Riga also had their reasons for embracing the Reformation. For the peasants of Latvia there was really no choice over what form of Christianity they participated in: For the peasant on the manor, those decisions came from the top down. Peasants were required to attend church on fear of reprisal. However, the Reformation was favorable to the native Latvians. Local Reformers took great pains to organize non-German congregations, which were provided with church buildings and pastors—for example, St. Jacob's church in Riga. The pastor of St. Jacob's—Sylvester Tegetmeier—has been called the "Father of the Livonian Reformation" for his work among the native Latvians. And the Lutherans emphasized the importance of teaching in the native language of the people. This brought with it the idea that the individual, common man was valuable before God.

Unlike many other Lutheran countries, Latvia did

not have an independent episcopal structure until the twentieth century, because Latvia itself was not independent until the twentieth century.

> The first bishop of the Evangelical Lutheran Church in Latvia was Karl Irbe who was consecrated to his office in 1922 by Archbishop Söderblom. At that time Söderblom suggested that the leader of the Latvian Church should have the title of archbishop. When Irbe voluntarily resigned his office as a result of an ecclesiastical-political conflict which concerned his defense of the independence of the Church, Teodors Grünbergs was chosen in 1932 as his successor. At this time the leadership of the Church adopted the title "archbishop" in order to give greater authority to the highest pastoral office, perhaps being influenced by the usage in the Swedish and Finnish Churches. However, Grünbergs was not consecrated according to the traditional forms; the laying on of hands was performed by some of the deans and other clergy immediately after the election in the assembly hall of the synod. Sometime later the oldest dean of the Church, assisted by the other deans, conducted the Service of Installation.*

Teodors Grīnbergs led the Latvian Church during World War II, at least during part of it. After the Soviet Union's second occupation (when the Germans were in retreat), Grīnbergs, and sixty per cent of the Lutheran clergy, had to flee and go into exile. The Red Army's advance was terrifying for the Church. The former archbishop "Kārlis Irbe was elected to lead the Church. Initially Irbe and others believed that co-operation with the new Soviet government would allow the church to retain some independence. However, this optimism

---

* *Episcopacy in the Lutheran Church?*, Ivar Asheim and Victor R. Gold, editors, (Fortress Press: Philadelphia, 1970) p. 136.

was destroyed with the arrest and deportation of Irbe and other active clergy."[*] The Soviet government oversaw the election of a new archbishop, Gustavs Tūrs, "though it was not possible to arrange the desired episcopal consecrations."[†] "In turn, he was succeeded by Pēteris Kleperis and Alberts Freijws both of whom, however, died shortly after their election and were never consecrated. From 1969 until 1983 the ELCL was led by Jānis Matulis."[‡] The lack of desired episcopal consecrations continued to be the case until the present archbishop of Latvia, Jānis Vanags. "Archbishop Jānis Vanags, first elected in 1993 at a special synod meeting following the untimely death of Archbishop Kārlis Gailītis in 1992, was consecrated bishop on August 29, 1993 by the Archbishop of"[§] Uppsala, Gunnar Weman. This would once again establish the so-called "apostolic succession" to Latvia.

APOSTOLIC SUCCESSION

The subject of apostolic succession is not strictly part of what is being considered in this paper, but it is so often a topic with regard to episcopacy that I would like to make a brief mention of it. Should Lutherans care about so called "apostolic succession"? For the most part, the answer should be, no. On the one hand, Lutherans have no problem obtaining or maintaining "apostolic succession" for the sake of tradition or for the sake of a weaker brother's conscience. However, Lutherans ought not be in the business of obtaining "apostolic succession" in order to make some other group or organization see them as legitimate. Chasing after Roman or Eastern or Anglican approval through so-called "apostolic succession" plays into the errors of these

* http://www.lelb.lv/en/?ct=history

† *Episcopacy in the Lutheran Church?*, p. 137.

‡ http://www.lelb.lv/en/?ct=history

§ http://en.wikipedia.org/wiki/Evangelical_Lutheran_Church_of_Latvia

churches. They make lists of successive office holders the test as to their own legitimacy, rather than an examination of doctrine that is passed on. If Roman "apostolic succession" can't keep Popes from kissing Korans or praying with imams in mosques, I fail to see its value. Likewise, Anglican apostolic succession hasn't stopped the Archbishop of Canterbury from being an honorary Druid. (I still like Hermann Sasse's treatment of the subject thus far in the *We Confess Anthology*.)

We should also note that there is no sort of "apostolic succession" that Lutherans can obtain that will make Rome or the East view their orders as valid. A Lutheran church body's "Lutheranism" invalidates any succession. Neither Rome nor the East recognize the Swedish succession, which is probably the only one worth having anyway, for a Lutheran, in regard to tradition.

The Church of Sweden has had "apostolic succession" since Stefan was consecrated Archbishop of Uppsala in A.D. 1164 by Pope Alexander III and the Archbishop of Lund, who was made Primate over Uppsala. Uppsala became independent of Lund when Folke Johansson Ängel was consecrated as Archbishop of Uppsala directly by Pope Gregory X in A.D. 1274. During the Reformation, Laurentius Petri was elected Archbishop of Uppsala by all the pastors of Sweden. "The Consecration took place on 22nd September 1531 at Stockholm, being performed by Petrus Magni, Bishop of Västeras, who had himself been confirmed and consecrated by the authority of Pope Clement VII in 1524."* "It was through this bishop that the Apostolic Succession was preserved in the Church of Sweden."† When Laurentius Petri Nericius died, the next archbishop of Uppsala, Laurentius Petri Gothus, maintained "apostolic succession" by having

* Eric E. Yelverton, *An Archbishop of the Reformation*, (The Epworth Press: London, 1958) p. 5.

† Ibid., p. 5 note.

as one of his consecrators, The bishop of Abo, Paul Juusten.

This succession has been passed to others. The Church of Finland and all three Baltic Lutheran churches also have their "apostolic succession" through Sweden. But, once again, neither the East nor Rome recognize this succession. Only the Anglicans are impressed with the Swedish pedigree.

Now, I'm not saying there is anything wrong with this Swedish succession in and of itself. The problem is with the false conclusions Rome or Canterbury come to with regard to it. If the ELDoNA were to have this Swedish succession made available to her (and I can't imagine that ever happening), it might be worth getting so long as she would not have to compromise herself in any way. The Swedish apostolic succession might be a nice bit of historic, traditional "window dressing," but certainly nothing essential.

It would seem to me that the difference between having the "historic episcopate" and simply episcopal polity is the matter of consecration at the hands of a bishop in the "historic episcopate." To see this "historic episcopate" as a necessary element for the Church would militate against Lutheran doctrine. But would episcopal consecration necessarily be a rejection of the doctrine, that there is but one office of the ministry, not multiple offices? Might not the Swedes have seen the Episcopal consecration as somehow a renewing of ordination and not a re-ordination? This is a question that requires more study.

Lutherans have historically embraced the office of bishop, but have embraced it as an grade within the office of the ministry by human rite. It does not seem that Lutherans could have another position on this issue. Even the Swedes, who supposedly have this "apostolic succession," do not view it as necessary in the way the Anglicans do. In 1922 the Swedish Bishops' Assembly wrote the following to the English:

> No particular organization of the Church and its ministry is instituted *iure divino.* Our Church cannot recognize any essential difference, *de iure divino,* of aim and authority between the two or three Orders into which the ministry of grace may have been divided, *iure humano,* for the benefit and welfare of the Church. The value of every organization of the *ministerium ecclesiasticum,* and of the Church in general, is only to be judged by its fitness and ability to become a pure vessel for the supernatural contents, and a perfect channel for the way of Divine Revelation unto mankind. That doctrine in no wise makes our Church indifferent to the organization and the forms of ministry which the cravings and experiences of the Christian community have produced under the guidance of the Spirit in the course of history. We do not only regard the peculiar forms and traditions of our Church with the reverence due to a venerable legacy from the past, but we recognize in them a blessing from the God of history accorded to us.*

This statement by the Swedish bishops clearly conforms to article 5 of the *Augsburg Confession,* where it says; "To obtain such faith God instituted the office of the ministry, ..."† There is but one office of the ministry by divine rite, not three offices. Men may sub-divide the one office into three in Christian freedom.

---

* *Episcopacy in the Lutheran Church?,* p. 134.

† *Augsburg Confession,* article 5, § 1., German text. Tappert, p. 31. (Jacobs, p. 38. Kolb/Wengert, p. 40.)

> The King set aside the rights of the Chapter of Uppsala Cathedral, and held an assembly of the clergy from the whole realm at Stockholm for the purpose of electing a new Archbishop. About one hundred and seventy priests took part in the election, and in the event no less than one hundred and fifty votes were cast for Laurentius Petri, a tremendous triumph for a young man of thirty-two years.*

This was the election of Laurentius Petri as Archbishop. The election functioned as his call to the see of Uppsala. Only a few years previously he had been studying in Wittenberg. When he came back to Sweden, the king appointed him to a professorship at the University of Uppsala, at the age of twenty-eight. It was at this time that he was ordained a priest.† In this case, the appointment by the king functioned as his call. He was a professor and a priest, and his call was to the university. He functioned in this capacity until one hundred-seventy bishops and priests gathered in Stockholm, at the king's request, and elected him archbishop. After his election, he was consecrated.

One objection to this form of calling a bishop is that no where do we see any lay participation in the calling process. And we rightly raise the question of the legitimacy of such a call. The blessed Martin Chemnitz wrote in his *Examen*; "…the apostolic history show[s] clearly that election or calling belongs in some way to the whole church, so that in their choosing and calling both presbyters and people are partners."‡ The main point that Chemnitz is making is that

* Eric E. Yelverton, p. 5.

† Ibid., p. 4.

‡ Martin Chemnitz, *Examination of the Council of Trent, Part II*, Fred Kramer, trans., (Concordia Publishing House: Saint Louis, 1978) pp. 708–709.

the clergy and the laity should not be pitted against one another, and the laity should not be disregarded. Chemnitz also warns against swinging in the direction of mob rule. He says:

> *But do Anabaptists do right, who entrust the whole right of calling to the common multitude (which they take the word* ekklesia *to mean), with the ministry and pious magistrate excluded?* By no means. For the church in each place is called, and is, the whole body embracing under Christ, the Head, all the members of that place. Eph 4:15–16; 1 Co 12:12–14, 27. Therefore as the call belongs not only to the ministry nor only to the magistrate, so also is it not to be made subject to the mere will [and] whim of the common multitude, for no part, with either one or both [of the others] excluded, is the church. But the call should be and remain in the power of the whole church, but with due order observed.*

Laurentius Petri also maintained the role of the three estates in his *Church Order* of 1571.

So, what of archbishop Petri's own election/call? Is it possible for a call to be legitimate without all three estates participating? And more to the point in our time, can it be legitimate without the participation of the laity?

Well, of course, the normal pattern of calling men to the office should include a role for the clergy and the laity. But is this some sort of iron-clad law, violation of which nullifies the call? The sainted professor Kurt Marquart briefly addressed this question. Of the standard of both lay and clerical participation in the call, he says:

---

* Martin Chemnitz, *Ministry, Word, and Sacraments: An Enchiridion,* Luther Poellot, ed., (Concordia Publishing House: Saint Louis, 1981) p. 34. (Note also that this Enchiridion was used by Chemnitz, as Superintendent/Bishop, in his examination of parish pastors.)

> The basic principle is simple and remains the same. But the applications allow of considerable variety in practice, depending on circumstances. Some classic examples will illustrate the point. If a group of captive Christian laymen, isolated in a desert, were to elect one of themselves to baptize, preach, and administer the Holy Supper, that man would be their pastor "as though he had been ordained by all the bishops and popes in the world" (Luther).*

Marquart also gave examples from Scripture of clergy standing in as representatives of the whole Church. He mentioned specifically Acts 14:23, "So when they had appointed elders in every church,… etc.," and he explained that in this passage "appointed" does not mean that the laity took a vote on the call. The word here "often means simply appoint, designate, set in place."† While Marquart acknowledged that simple appointments of clergy are valid, he came to his main point:

> On the other hand, it would be absurd to assume that either Paul and Barnabas (Acts 14:23) or Titus (Tit. 1:5) were able or willing autocratically to impose unacceptable ministers on unwilling churches. Fraternal mutual consultation, accommodation, and cooperation are simply the self-evident rule of life in the New Testament Church (Rom. 14:1-3; I Cor. 9:19-22; Phil. 2:1-11; I Pet. 5:3)."‡

So, it would be possible and legitimate for a ministerium to call or elect a bishop without active lay participation (e.g.

---

* Kurt E. Marquart, *The Church and Her Fellowship, Ministry, and Governance,* Confessional Lutheran Dogmatics, vol. IX, (The International Foundation for Lutheran Confessional Research: Fort Wayne, Indiana, 1990) p. 147.

† Ibid., p. 146.

‡ Ibid.

voting), so long as he is not objected to by the laity. If the laity give implicit approval, by simply not objecting, the spirit of the call is not violated. The main point is not to shove an unwanted bishop or priest down the laity's throat, so to speak.

And very often in the history of the Lutheran Church the calling of a bishop (or even a parish pastor) has been given over to a group of clergy, with the addition sometimes of a few knowledgeable laymen. This was certainly the case for the Church of Sweden. Laurentius Petri's *Church Order* of 1571 describes "concerning the election of a bishop."

> In former times it hath been the custom that the whole commonality should elect the bishops as well as the other servants of the Church. Albeit this is proper, where it can be done in a Christian manner; and it must surely be accomplished by an election according to the order of the Church. Nevertheless circumstances are now otherwise in these respects both that, the dioceses of Bishops having grown larger than they were at the first, all men cannot meet for such business, and likewise also that there are few of the common folk who can have any knowledge of the persons who would best serve in such an office. Therefore shall the election of Bishops be given into the hands of some appointed persons of the estate of the clergy and others who are in some degree experienced in this matter and bound by the duty of oath, that they shall elect and nominate him who in the sight of God seemeth to be most fitted for such an office.*

I'm not saying that the laity should not be involved in the election of a bishop. I am simply saying that their lack of active participation does not invalidate the call. The Church

* Yelverton, p. 141.

definitely has the power and authority to call bishops and parish priests, but how the Church calls, how it is configured, how the process proceeds, is open to much latitude. If we do not acknowledge that, then for much of our Lutheran Church's history, men have not been called. Even the Reformers themselves would have invalid calls. For example, the estate of the laity never participated in Luther's call. The great Lutheran theologian, Johann Gerhard, received his call to the superintendency of Heldburg from the prince of Coburg's chancellor, Volckmar Scherer.* Certainly we must allow for flexibility in how calls are given.

THE AUTHORITY OF AN ELDoNA BISHOP

One of the criticisms that we in the ELDoNA have heard about our episcopal polity is that it is not a traditional episcopacy; that is, the parishes of the diocese are not under the authority of the bishop. Parishes are affiliated or associated with the diocese, but it is the pastors who are members of the diocese. Therefore, Bishop Heiser cannot directly discipline any parish; he can only call the pastor to obedience. Some have claimed that this is an innovation for episcopacy, and it makes it a rather weak form of episcopacy. And we readily admit, that is true. In our ELDoNA charter we talk about how the bishop may remove a parish pastor from the diocese for some sin. However, "We acknowledge and affirm that such a removal from the diocese does not remove a man from his call; congregations shall be encouraged to follow their congregational constitutions and bylaws in all such matters."† The bishop can do nothing else but remove a pastor from the diocese.

---

* Erdmann Rudolph Fischer, *The Life of John Gerhard*, (Repristination Press: Malone, Texas, 2001) p. 52.

† ELDoNA Charter. (See Appendix.)

When forming the ELDoNA we intentionally limited the power and scope of the episcopacy for some very practical reasons. I believe that those who have criticized us for not instituting a more medieval type of episcopacy do not understand what they are proposing. Medieval bishops had civil powers which simply do not exist today. Today, if a parish is abusing its pastor, the bishop could admonish them that they are in the wrong, and call them to repentance, but he has no punitive powers. And in our twenty-first century American context, how could there be? We do not have the power of the State to bring to bear on the parish, as a medieval bishop might. Nor do we have the power to coerce by seizing property. Even if such powers were desirable (and they are not), they are not attainable in our current context. What should we do? Should we attempt to get all the parishes of our diocese to sign over the deeds to their property to the bishop? Fat chance getting a bunch of Americans to do that, let alone when the laity who have largely come from a Synodical Conference background. And we would never want to put ourselves in the position of throwing little old ladies out of their church buildings. We knew right from the beginning of the ELDoNA that these were aspects of medieval episcopal power with which we wanted nothing to do.

An ELDoNA bishop conducts visitations of the clergy to examine their doctrine and life. (In a year and a half I've already received two such visitations. I never had any such thing in the LCMS.) And the bishop conducts all ordinations, and he does that, *de jure humano*, for the sake of unity. We view our bishop as *primus inter pares*, first among equals. He sets for us a general vision for the future of the diocese, but we can all help shape our future. Nothing in our polity ought to be seen as Romanizing or tyrannizing. We have simply tried to establish an evangelical episcopacy in our twenty-first century, American context. We believe we have honored the spirit of the *Apology*, article fourteen, as best we could.

I am honored to be allowed to speak to you today, and I admire all of you for having the courage to follow through with your commitment to the Lutheran Confessions, even when it's hard to do. I would like to extend to all of you the good will of the Evangelical Lutheran Diocese of North America. And I hope and pray that we can come closer together as church bodies. Thank you.

Call, Consecration, and Episcopacy*

The Evangelical Lutheran Diocese of North America has embarked on an experiment that is almost totally unique in the context of American Lutheranism: We are creating an episcopally ordered church body from nothing. This being the case, we will inevitably find ourselves coming to deeper understanding about episcopacy in the midst of living out that reality. In other words, we are forming some of our practices, procedures, and traditions "on the fly" since we have no confessional Lutheran examples of such a polity in our immediate context. Questions have arisen over the last few years, as to the details of how a Lutheran episcopacy works. What is the nature of the bishop's call? How is a Lutheran bishop different than a Roman or Anglican bishop? Can a Lutheran bishop have "apostolic succession"? And how would one consecrate a Lutheran bishop? Since the Evangelical Lutheran Diocese of North America is committed to "the restoration of the historic, preferred polity—that is, the offices of Bishop, Presbyter, and Deacon—within the one divinely-established office of the ministry,"† we need to further refine our understanding of this polity in order to be able to discuss it with those Lutherans who are outside our diocese.

---

* Presented at the Theological Colloquium of The Evangelical Lutheran Diocese of North America (14 May 2009).

† Malone Theses, 06 June 2006, Thesis number six.

THE CALL AND CALLS

To begin with, I want to briefly explore the idea of the multi-faceted call or multiple calls to the one office. The Lutheran Church has always taught that there is an office of the holy ministry and that qualified men are called by God, through the Church, to fill that office. The Lutheran Church has also always taught that there is but one office of the holy ministry—not two or three offices—and that any division of that one office into different grades is purely by human arrangement. These are givens in our theology. But some of the details of the call have been carried out in different ways. How many of the functions of the office of the ministry does one engage in, in any particular call? For example, deacons, while possessing all the authority that is inherent in the office of the ministry, willingly give up some of the exercise of that authority to the presbyter under whom they serve. And the limited exercise of the office of the ministry is part of the very call the deacon receives. A deacon's call to be a deacon does not diminish in any way his call into the office of the holy ministry.

Every call is a call to the office of the holy ministry no matter what the parameters of the exercise of the office are. No matter whether the call is for a deacon, a bishop, a seminary professor, a missionary, or any other grade of the holy ministry, the call is a call to the office of the keys. This is certain.

But unlike the situation that we were all familiar with in the Lutheran Church–Missouri Synod, the ELDoNA's polity gives rise to a new question about multiple calls. Can a man have multiple calls to the office of the holy ministry? Can a man, for example, be called to be a deacon and be called to be a seminary professor at the same time? Certainly Lutheran Church history would seem to answer, yes. This situation of multiple calls appears to have been the case in the life of one of our greatest church fathers, the blessed Martin Chemnitz.

Martin Chemnitz's life in Braunschweig began with an interesting combination of positions. "[T]he same year that he became a faculty member at Wittenberg, Chemnitz received an invitation from his old friend of Königsberg days, Joachim Mörlin, informing him that the office of coadjutor was vacant, along with the pastorate at Martin Church, and he wanted Chemnitz to fill both positions."* On September 28, 1554, Martin Chemnitz accepted the call. This certainly seemed to be a multiple position call or multiple, simultaneous calls to the office of the ministry in Braunschweig. But this situation with Martin Chemnitz is not an isolated anomaly. This sort of multiple position call or calls was also evident in the life of Johann Gerhard. We find that he also had such multiple calls. In the year 1606, "[o]n the recommendation of Wolfgang Heider, professor of logic and ethics at the academy of Jena, it happened that Dr. Volckmar Scherer, chancellor of Coburg, offered John Gerhard the office of archdeacon and professor of theology at the gymnasium of Coburg."† After trying to argue that he was too young and inexperienced for the positions offered him, he finally relented and accepted the call. "On August 24, after delivering the sermon, Melchior Bischoff, bishop of Coburg, crowned him [Gerhard] with the rite of ordination, as they call it. ...The pastors of twenty six parishes were present for

* J.A.O. Preus, *The Second Martin: The Life and Theology of Martin Chemnitz*, (Concordia Publishing House: St. Louis, 1994) p. 99.
Note: A "coadjutor" is a bishop who is an assistant to the diocesan bishop. He is nearly a co-bishop with the diocesan bishop and usually succeeds the diocesan bishop.

† Erdmann Rudolph Fischer, *The Life of John Gerhard*, (Repristination Press: Malone, Texas, 2001) p. 51.
Note: An "archdeacon" is the assistant and representative of the bishop. The archdeacon administers a subdivision of a diocese. Unlike a coadjutor, he does not automatically succeed to the bishopric.

this, and they promised their obligatory obedience to this new supervisor of theirs."* That this ordination referred to two different positions is confirmed in the footnote to the above quotation. It says, "With regard to the ordination of John Gerhard … called as he was into the office of superintendent and pastor…[etc.]"† Was Gerhard's call one call for two different positions, or two simultaneous calls? What if he had first been called as a parish pastor or professor, and then six months later he had been called to the superintendency in addition to the first call? This would hardly be an unthinkable scenario, and no doubt, happened often. Is Gerhard in two or more offices? There is but one office of the ministry, so clearly he was not in two offices. He must have occupied the same office of the keys through these different calls. These cases from our history seem to indicate to us that the Lutheran Fathers thought of it as perfectly legitimate to have multiple calls or a multiple graded call. No matter how many calls one had, one was always only called into the one office of the ministry.

Applying these historic precedents to our circumstances is our task. We don't have civil authorities as part of our calling process, but we do have a multi-fold office as part of our structure. In our situation, the Reverend James Heiser was called by the Church (specifically, Salem Lutheran Church of Malone, Texas) to be her pastor. He accepted that call to the holy ministry. Many years later, when the Evangelical Lutheran Diocese of North America was formed,

* Ibid. p. 54. It is interesting to note that on the same page of Fischer's book it says, "His serene highness John Casimir had promoted Gerhard to the superintendency [επισκοπη] of Heldburg…"

† Ibid. p. 64. See also Gerhard's *Sacred Meditations*. In the introduction by Charles Albert, he says; "In 1606, the same year in which the *Meditationes Sacræ* appeared, he [Gerhard] accepted the duke of Coberg's invitation to a professorship in the Coberg Gymnasium and to the superintendency of Heldburg." Johann Gerhard, *Sacred Meditations,* (Repristination Press: Malone, TX, 2000) p. 8.

Pastor Heiser was called by the Church (specifically, the entire diocese) to be bishop. The call to be bishop did not end his call to be pastor of Salem Lutheran Church. And his call to the bishopric of the ELDoNA was in fact, a divine call, just as Chemnitz and Gerhard received divine calls to their respective bishoprics while serving simultaneously as parish pastors or professors. It would be hard to imagine Martin Chemnitz not appealing to his call if his authority were challenged in any of the grades of call he held. Though some outside of our diocese might find our multi-ranked calls difficult to grasp, we stand on solid Lutheran precedent.

CONSECRATION, ORDINATION, INSTALLATION

In addition to the divine call a bishop receives to his office, there is a ceremony of placing him in his office that has been observed throughout the history of the Church. This naturally parallels the call and ordination of the presbyter. Just as the parish priest/pastor is called and ordained to his office, the bishop is also called and then placed into office in a liturgical ceremony. The question for us is: what is that ceremony of placing into office for a Lutheran bishop? Is it ordination? Is it consecration? Is it installation? There do seem to be subtle differences between these terms when we look at how various churches employ them. Roman Catholic, Orthodox, and Anglican Christians see themselves as not only installing their bishops, but consecrating or ordaining them as well. In this view, an installation would be a simple public placing into office of a bishop-elect, nothing more. In a consecration (or ordination, as it is sometimes called), the intention would be to do more than merely install the bishop-elect. A consecration involves prayer for the imparting of the grace of the Holy Ghost, a laying on of hands, and (according to an Anglican or Roman view) an intention to confer a specific and unique gift or office. And additionally, in the

Roman view, one would have to be in communion with the Roman Church. But how do Lutherans view this placing into office ceremony? Are Lutherans against any kind of episcopal ordination or consecration? Can one be a bishop without ordination/consecration? In light of the fact that Swedish Lutherans have had bishops for their entire existence, rather than elected "presidents,"* is consecration of a bishop something that Lutherans have done historically, and what does it mean? One way to begin answering these questions is to look at the historic Swedish Church Orders to find out what they have done in the past.

Church Orders (*Kirchenordnungen*) are ecclesiastical regulations that are enforced by the State. In a number of European countries, the Lutheran Church was the official church of the State, and the State had an interest in maintaining order and uniformity in the Church. Functionally, Church Orders are what succeeded Roman Canon Law in those lands which had embraced the Reformation. Church Orders "usually open with a statement of the doctrinal position of the country or state or city [*Credenda*], followed by regulations concerning the liturgy, the appointment of church officers, and the whole administration of various congregations included in the respective jurisdiction [*Agenda*]."† With regard to Church Orders in Sweden, "the *Swedish Church Ordinance* of 1571 was the first complete Swedish church order following the Swedish Reformation in the 1520's. The main originator of the ordinance was Archbishop Laurentius Petri."‡ So, we should start in the *Agenda* of this Church Order to determine the nature of the consecration of a bishop in the Church of Sweden. But first, for the sake of thorough-

---

* Though it should be noted that the Swedish Church had bishops and superintendents simultaneously for many generations.

† Erwin L. Lueker, ed., *Lutheran Cyclopedia,* (Concordia Publishing House: St. Louis, 1954) p. 230.

‡ http://en.wikipedia.org/wiki/Swedish_Church_Ordinance_1571

ness, I'll briefly mention the order immediately preceding the Reformation.

In the Swedish Church, there had been a continuous use of a rite of consecration of a bishop from before the Church Order of 1571, and it continued until the Ordinal* of 1809. Before the Church Order of 1571, the Roman orders were used in some fashion or other. For example, we know how Archbishop Petri's episcopal consecrator was himself consecrated. Petrus Magni was the bishop who consecrated Laurentius Petri. "The Roman Pontifical was used at the consecration of *Petrus Magni* to the see of Westeräs. This took place in Rome, May 1, 1524."† Clearly Rome's understanding of consecration was that the bishop-elect was being given some divine gift in his consecration. Laurentius Petri was consecrated, in some manner or other, according to this old form. "The precise forms are not known, but there is testimony of importance that cope, staff, mitre, and unction were used."‡

So then, in regard to the Lutheran orders, Laurentius Petri Nericius was Archbishop of Uppsala for forty-two years (1531-1573), and he worked on, and published, the first Lutheran Church Order. "The old Archbishop published his *Kyrko-Ordning* in 1571. It was adopted by the Diet at Upsala in 1572."§ In this Church Order, written by Petri himself we find the rite entitled, "*The Way to Ordain a Bishop-Elect*," which reads as follows: "On some Sunday or other Holy Day before the Mass begins, the Bishop to be ordained (*Ordinandus Episcopus*) comes before the altar in surplice and cope,

---

* In liturgy, an ordinal is a book that gives the ordo (ritual and rubrics) for celebrations.

† Ibid. p. 9. The Roman Pontifical (*Pontificale Romanum*) is the Roman Catholic liturgical book that contains the rites performed by bishops.

‡ Ibid.

§ Ibid. p. 10.

..."[*] Note here the phrase "... Bishop to be ordained ...". Archbishop Petri used the word "ordained" when speaking of placing the bishop-elect into his office. The rite continues with the rubric:

> ...the Ordainer with the other Bishops who are present lay their hands on the head of Ordinandi, the Ordinator first saying, 'Let us pray... We, therefore, beseech Thee heartily, that Thou wouldest mercifully look upon this Thy servant whom we have chosen and taken to this service and Bishop's office, giving him Thy Holy Spirit, that he may truly and powerfully carry out Thy holy work, teach and rebuke with all meekness and wisdom.'[†]

In this consecration rite for a Swedish bishop, the language of consecration/ordination is clearly used. Phrases and words such as "Bishop to be ordained," "Ordainer," "Ordinandi," and "Ordinator," along with the prayer to give the Holy Spirit to the one being ordained, demonstrate the nature of the rite of placing the bishop in office in this 1571 Church Order. The man thus consecrated was regarded as a bishop in the Church of Sweden, and it is believed, vested like a bishop. He is more than merely installed, in that he is given the gift of the Holy Ghost and the gift of his office in this liturgical ceremony. And with regard to vestments, "The rubrics are not regarded as exhaustively descriptive, and, while mitre and staff are there not mentioned, they were, according to tradition, always, or almost always, used."[‡]

So, here, in this rite, we have the laying on of hands and prayer for the gift of the Holy Ghost. This certainly seems like more than a simple installation. Perhaps we could

---

* G. Mott Williams, *The Church of Sweden and The Anglican Communion,* (The Young Churchman Co.: Milwaukee, 1910) p. 12.

† Ibid. pp. 14–15.

‡ Ibid. p. 10.

call this "installation plus," because of the language used and the gifts given. This concept of ordaining a bishop and conveying a divine gift to him is also confirmed by the 1571 rite for "The Election of Bishops." In that rite it says, "When he is thus approved, confirmed, and with open letters set in the diocese, he shall be publicly ordained by some other Bishop or Bishops in the Cathedral or some other convenient church, by the laying on of hands."* There seems to be no ambiguity as to the nature of the consecration of a bishop in Petri's 1571 Church Order: The language is that of ordination/consecration, and whatever that means, it includes the laying on of hands and the imparting of the gift of the Holy Ghost.

This 1571 Church Order remains in effect until a new one replaces it in 1686, some 115 years later. "In 1686 there were very material changes made in the Church law, in the *Kyrko-ordning,* and some additions to the Confession of Faith."† However, the significant elements are still there, that is, it is still a rite that includes the laying on of hands and the impartation of the Holy Ghost, and the language of consecration/ordination is still used. Some of the significant instructions in this Church Order are as follows; "1. On some Sunday or other holy day when the Bishop's ordination (*vigning*) shall occur, …"‡ And, "14. When they have risen the Archbishop and assistants lay their hands on the new Bishop's head, saying, Our Father, etc."§

The Rt. Rev. Dr. G. Mott Williams, Anglican Bishop of Marquette, Michigan comments:

> It will be noticed that this Ordinal has been a good deal strengthened: 1. By designating the Arch-

* Ibid. pp. 11–12.

† Ibid. p. 17.

‡ Ibid.

§ Ibid. p. 19.

> bishop as the ordinator, which he always was before without reasons for the contrary. 2. By specifying several episcopal assistants. 3. By express words of authoritative delivery, on behalf of God and His Church, and by the use of a particular vestment allied in Sweden with the Episcopate, the cope. No mention is made of the mitre, but it appears to have been used, with the cross and staff.*

This Church Order seems to be the high point of consecration-type installation. It maintains all the consecration aspects of the 1571 order and makes them stronger.

This Church Order remains in effect for 123 years, until 1809. Then we come to the Swedish Ordinal of 1809. Here we have for the first time the word "install" (*inställa).* Here is an excerpt from that Ordinal: "At the end of divine service, the act begins with a suitable psalm, during which there advance to the altar first two priests wearing chasubles, then the Bishop to be *installed* (set) in office, …"† However, this change of vocabulary does not signal any real change in practice. The Archbishop still prays for a gift of grace for the bishop being set in office. The Ordinal says,

> *"…Look, Lord, in mercy upon this Thy servant, who comes before Thy face to be set in the Bishop's office. We pray Thee with confiding hearts, Give him grace, that, according to Thy holy intentions, and agreeably to Thy will, he may further the great purpose which Thou hast aimed at through the Teaching Office, the eternal salvation of souls. … Give him grace narrowly to prove and ordain skilled teachers for the service of the Church* [etc.]*"*‡

---

* Ibid. pp. 19–20.

† Ibid. p. 21.

‡ Ibid. pp. 21–22.

The laying on of hands is performed and the Ordinal continues as follows; *"The Archbishop and assistants now vest the Bishop with the cope, whereupon they lay their hands on the Bishop's head..."*[*] The new bishop even wears a mitre. One might think because of the new word "install" that here we have a break from the concept of consecration in favor of some lesser concept of installation. But Anglican bishop Williams argues that consecration is assumed in this "installation." He says, "for a Bishop is never otherwise installed except at his consecration."[†] Though the word "installation" is used here, the form of a consecration remains. The bishop-elect is vested with the symbols of the office of bishop. A prayer for the imparting of grace is offered. And grace is requested specifically for his functions as bishop, that is, proving and ordaining teachers for the Church. And then, of course, the laying on of hands is maintained.

The Ordinal of 1809 remained in effect for 72 years. In its replacement of 1881, there are not very many significant changes. One point to be noted is that in the Ordinal of 1881, "the word *inviga* is used in the closing part of the long rubric as the precise equivalent of *inställa*."[‡] So, we see that not only are the words "ordain" and "install" used as synonyms in this order, but this use of language very much helps our interpretation of the language used in the 1809 Ordinal.

This brief survey of the Swedish Church Orders gives us some idea of the nature of the rite of placing a bishop into office. This consecrating of bishops has been the practice of the Church of Sweden through its entire history, and is the practice of the Church of Sweden to this day. Additionally, the Lutheran Churches of Finland, Estonia, and Latvia have historically followed the Swedish practice and have revived it in our present day as well. This is an amazingly wide-

* Ibid. p. 24.

† Ibid. p. 25.

‡ Ibid. p. 27.

spread historical precedence for a type of episcopal consecration in the Lutheran Church. So, the existence of episcopal consecration—or a consecration-type installation—in the history of the Lutheran Church cannot be denied. Its validity as a Lutheran practice would also seem hard to deny, from an historical perspective. Too many Lutherans have consecrated bishops for too long to ignore this practice.

So, there can be no denying that there has been long precedence for Lutheran episcopal consecrations. But, so what? What does this practice of consecration mean? What about the doctrine that there is but one office of the ministry? How does that affect the concept of episcopal consecration?

There are a couple of issues with the Swedish consecration rite (even back to 1571) that call into question the true nature of the act. First of all, though the Swedish ritual for consecrating a bishop closely follows the ritual for the consecration of a parish priest, there is one difference.* In the 1571 *Kyrko-ordning* (Church Order), under the section "The Manner of Ordaining Priests," we find this declaration by the ordaining bishop:

> "AND I, BY THE AUTHORITY ENTRUSTED TO ME ON GOD'S BEHALF BY HIS CHURCH FOR THIS PURPOSE, COMMIT UNTO YOU (THEE) THE OFFICE OF PRIEST, IN THE NAME OF THE FATHER, AND OF THE SON, AND OF THE HOLY SPIRIT, *AMEN*."†

This declaration says that the priest has a God-given office. But what about the ordaining of a bishop? There was no such analogous declaration in the ritual for the or-

* I wish to acknowledge the enormous help I received from Dr. William Tighe of Muhlenberg College on this point. He graciously and generously guided my research through a personal correspondence.

† Eric E. Yelverton, *An Archbishop of the Reformation,* (The Epworth Press: London, 1958) p. 134.

daining of a bishop, saying that his office was God-given. This, seemingly intentional, lack of declaration brings forward questions about what was the intention of the Swedish Church in consecrating bishops? The lack of this declaration is only magnified when in the Ordinal of 1686 a declaration was added to the ritual of ordaining a bishop which said:

> "AND I, BY THE AUTHORITY ENTRUSTED TO ME BY THE KING'S SOVEREIGNTY (*FULLMAKT*) FOR THIS PURPOSE, COMMIT UNTO THEE THE OFFICE OF BISHOP IN THE CHURCH OF SWEDEN, IN THE NAME OF THE FATHER, AND OF THE SON, AND OF THE HOLY SPIRIT, *AMEN*."

This declaration might seem to say that the royal commission made the bishop; that this was a man-given office, which would change the entire nature of the office, and be a significant factor in determining what such a consecration was.

This difference in the rites between ordaining parish priests on the one hand, and bishops on the other, tell us, at the very least, that the Swedish Lutherans clearly saw the office of bishop not as a separate and distinct office from any other grade of the office of the ministry. The difference in the two rites shows that the Swedes thought of the bishop's office as a man-made grade within the office of the keys.

There is other evidence that the Swedish Lutherans saw the various grades of the office as just that, and not separate offices. Dr. William Tighe reports,

> Between the 1560s and the 1770s, in addition to the 7 (later 8) bishops there were also 5 "superintendents." These "superintendents" were simply appointed, and received no form of "ordination" or "installation" at the hands of either bishops or other su-

> perintendents, and on those rare occasions when a superintendent became a bishop he did not receive any form of episcopal consecration, which is also what happened in 1772 when all the remaining superintendents were given the title of bishop -- and yet these superintendents could themselves ordain and perform all the other functions of bishops. Moreover, (1) although ordination became an episcopal monopoly in Sweden from 1786 onwards, prior to that date a bishop, with the permission of the king, could delegate ordinations to the Dean of his cathedral, and on some occasions the king himself conferred permission to perform ordinations upon pastors, such as royal chaplains, and (2) it became routine in the 18th century for bishops-elect to perform ordinations immediately after their appointment and before themselves receiving episcopal consecration—consecrations which, in some cases, did not happen until some years after the bishop's appointment and which, in the case of one bishop, who refused to be consecrated, never happened at all.*

There certainly seems to be a mixed track record in the history of the Church of Sweden. While some—Archbishop Laurentius Petri, for example—have arranged for genuine consecration of bishops, others have fought against such consecrations. On top of that, both sides in that disagreement of practice acknowledge that there is but one office of the ministry. It certainly seems that the Swedes—according to their best leading lights—have, historically, intended to establish something akin to an historic bishop as opposed to a president who fills a term and is re-elected in a purely administrative fashion, but at the same time, they were not mimicking the concept of a medieval Roman bishop. They were practicing a genuine consecration/ordination

* Personal correspondence.

of bishops (in those cases where they did practice it) while recognizing this grade of the office as man-made. This is a uniquely Lutheran approach to the episcopal office. How does this Lutheran concept of the office line up with other concepts of the office?

THEOLOGICAL PERSPECTIVES

What is a consecration? What is it to Romanists and Anglicans? What is it to Lutherans? For Roman Catholics and Anglicans, consecration must include the laying-on of hands with prayer by a consecrator who is in a distinct office of bishop, and who is in a recognized succession of such bishops. Now, Lutherans would have no problem with the laying-on of hands and prayer, as they regularly do this in installations. And "apostolic succession" would be a matter of *adiaphora* (as it is to the Swedes). But if consecration must have as a component, the recognition that the bishop-elect was being placed into a distinct office from that of the parish priest, we are at an impasse for Lutherans because we are constrained by our Confessions. The *Treatise on the Power and Primacy of the Pope* says:

> By the confession of all, even our adversaries, it is evident that this power [of the keys] belongs by divine right to all who preside over the churches, whether they are called pastors, presbyters, or bishops. … Jerome therefore teaches that the distinction between the grades of bishop and presbyter (or pastor) is by human authority.*

With this doctrine, i.e. of the one office of the keys, it seems that Lutherans have taken themselves out of the whole

* *Treatise on the Power and Primacy of the Pope*, § 61 and 63. Theodore G. Tappert, ed., *The Book of Concord*, (Fortress Press: Philadelphia, 1959) pp. 330–331.

"valid consecration" and "apostolic succession" conversation. Dr. Hermann Sasse made this point about the connection between episcopal consecration and "apostolic succession" quite well. He said, "If one accepts the Roman view, then the apostolic succession makes some sense: The power to make the sacrifice of the Mass and the power to absolve is bestowed. If one does not accept this view, then there is no apostolic succession."* The ideas of a unique, divinely instituted episcopal office and apostolic succession really hang together and Lutherans have rejected this Roman view from the very beginning. And with regard to the idea of one office of the ministry verses multiple offices and how such an office relates to "apostolic succession," Pope Benedict XVI agrees with Hermann Sasse, and of course, goes even further. When known as Joseph Cardinal Ratzinger, he said that such "apostolic succession" that Anglicans or Lutherans have is "apocryphal." He said:

> Wherever such "high-church" ordinations are conferred or received thus "apocryphally," the fundamental nature of the imposition of hands has been totally misunderstood. Regardless of the positive reasons that occasion it, it expresses, in such cases, either a liturgical romanticism or a canonical tutiorism.

Ratzinger then goes on to explain:

> In truth, the imposition of hands with the accompanying prayer for the Holy Spirit is not a rite that can be separated from the Church or by which one can bypass the rest of the Church and dig one's own private channel to the apostles.†

* *We Confess Anthology,* (Concordia Publishing House: Saint Louis, 1999) p. 103.

† Joseph Cardinal Ratzinger, *Principles of Catholic Theology: Building Stones for a fundamental Theology,* (Ignatius Press: San Francisco, 1987).

The Second Vatican Council agrees with this when it proclaimed:

> "The college or body of bishops has…no authority unless united with the Roman Pontiff,…Together with their head, the Supreme Pontiff, and never apart from him, they [the bishops] have supreme and full authority over the universal Church; but this power cannot be exercised without the agreement of the Roman Pontiff."*

The only partial exception Rome seems to give to this standard is that they recognize the Eastern churches as churches and Rome recognizes their "apostolic succession." But "Protestant" churches are not churches in the strict sense and so they can have no succession. The point is that Rome does not recognize "Protestant" orders because they are "Protestant" and outside the true Church, as they conceive it.

Rome rejected Anglican orders in 1896 with the Papal Encyclical *Apostolicae Curae*. Then, Pope Leo XIII said, "we pronounce and declare that ordinations carried out according to the Anglican rite have been, and are, absolutely null and utterly void."† The concept of "apostolic succession" cannot exist apart from a distinct office of bishop, nor can it exist for the Roman or Eastern churches apart from communion with the Roman or Eastern churches. And from our side of this division, Dr. Sasse agrees that arguing for perfectly rigorous rites and unbroken strings of succession to the see of Rome misses the point. Sasse says, "This is also not the direction of the Roman arguments against the valid-

---

Quoted in *Apostolic Succession in an ecumenical Context*, (Alba House: New York, pp. 78–79).

* Dogmatic Constitution On The Church, Vatican II, *Lumen Gentium*, 21 November, 1964, paragraph 22. Quoted from *Vatican II: The Conciliar and Post Conciliar Documents*, Ed. Austin Flannery, O.P., p. 375.

† http://www.papalencyclicals.net/Leo13/l13curae.htm

ity of Anglican orders. As we have seen, these attach to the faulty formula of ordination and the lack of the intention to make the one ordained into a priest in the Roman Catholic sense. Against these considerations the laying on of hands, be it ever so canonical, is of no avail."* The Vatican would not see Lutheran "apostolic succession" from Uppsala any more favorably than it does the Anglican variety from Canterbury.

Now, with regard to the Anglican Church, the Anglicans would not, of course, require fellowship with Rome in order to recognize orders as authentic, but they would require that a Church intend to ordain into a distinct episcopal office. The three distinct offices of deacon, presbyter, and bishop are part of the very fiber of Anglicanism. Episcopate and Prayer Book define who they are. It is hard to see how an Anglican view of the episcopate can be reconciled with a Lutheran one given our confessional commitments, but throughout the twentieth and twenty-first centuries they seem to have done it.

RECOGNITION OF ORDERS

One of the most amazing developments in twentieth century ecumenism has been the mutual recognition of orders between the Anglicans and Lutherans. As far back as 1888, the Anglicans made efforts to establish full communion with the Church of Sweden.† The Anglicans formally pursued an alliance with the Church of Sweden in 1909, after the Swedes sent greetings to the Anglicans.‡ The Lambeth Conference requested that the Archbishop of Canterbury appoint a commission to correspond further with the Swedish Church through the Archbishop of Uppsala on the pos-

* Hermann Sasse, *We Confess Anthology*, p. 104.

† Lambeth Conference 1888, Resolution 14. Lambeth Conference 1897, Resolution 39.

‡ Lambeth Conference 1908, Resolution 74.

sibility of such an alliance. This commission was assembled and met with the Swedish delegation in Uppsala, Sweden on 21–23 September 1909, and also continued their talks after this meeting. The Anglicans finally offered their conclusions to the Archbishop of Canterbury on 25 January 1911. They concluded:

> (1) That the succession of bishops has been maintained unbroken by the Church of Sweden, and that it has a true conception of the episcopal office, though it does not as a whole consider the office to be so important as most English Churchmen do; [And] (2) That the office of priest is also rightly conceived as a divinely instituted instrument for the ministry of the Word and Sacraments, and that it has been in intention handed on throughout the whole history of the Church of Sweden. The change in language introduced in 1811, which continued in use until 1894, does not appear to us to have vitiated the intention, when regard is paid to other documents which remained in authority and throughout testified to that intention. For example, this intention is manifested in the *Augustana Confessio*, Articles V. and VII., and elsewhere, both in the Prayer Book itself and in the Church Law.*

The conclusions of this commission were approved by the Lambeth Conference of 1920 which stated:

> The Conference welcomes the Report of the Commission appointed after the last Conference entitled "The Church of England and the Church of Swe-

* "The Church of England and the Church of Sweden" Report of the Commission Appointed by the Archbishop of Canterbury In Pursuance of Resolution 74 of the Lambeth Conference of 1908 On the Relation of the Anglican Communion to the Church of Sweden.
http://anglicanhistory.org/lutherania/conference1909.html

> den," and, accepting the conclusions there maintained on the succession of bishops of the Church of Sweden and the conception of the priesthood set forth in its standards, recommends that members of that Church, qualified to receive the sacrament in their own Church, should be admitted to Holy Communion in ours. It also recommends that on suitable occasions permission should be given to Swedish ecclesiastics to give addresses in our churches.*

But the conclusions of this commission and conference ought to be examined. As has been noted, the Commission appointed by the Archbishop of Canterbury met with a delegation from the Church of Sweden in Uppsala in 1909. The report of this Anglican commission came to some conclusions that are problematic for confessional Lutherans. Section or topic four was problematic for confessional Lutherans. Topic number four was entitled *Doctrinal Force and Authority of the "Confessio Augustana" in the Church of Sweden.* The commission reports that the representatives of the Church of Sweden told them that both the Church and its ministers were bound to the *Book of Concord.* The Anglican commission, presumably knowing what was taught in the *Concordia,* asked the following;

> We inquired on whom these standards are binding, and whether any latitude was allowed in the interpretation of them. We were informed that they are generally considered to be formally binding on the clergy only. The question in the ordination of priests now [after 1904] is: "Will you, according to your best understanding and conscience, purely and clearly preach God's Word as it is given to us in Holy Scripture and as our Church's confessional books

* Lambeth Conference 1920, Resolution 24, "Reunion of Christendom." http://www.lambethconference.org/resolutions/1920/1920-24.cfm

> witness concerning the same?" It was explained that the words "according to your best understanding and conscience" were introduced in 1904 by way of expressing more clearly the evangelical conception of adherence to the Symbola of the Church.*

It is clear that the groundwork was laid in 1904 to circumvent the authority of the *Book of Concord.* The members of the Swedish delegation actively participated in a deception about the nature and authority of the *Book of Concord* in the Church of Sweden (at least from 1593 until 1904). Section or topic seven of the commission's report clearly lays out the Lutheran understanding of the office of the ministry—even extensively quoting Archbishop Laurentius Petri—and yet the commission could conclude that the Church of Sweden "has a true conception of the episcopal office." This could not be true according to the Anglican conception of the episcopal office. Section seven said that the Lutherans believed that "No particular organization of the Church and of its ministry is instituted *jure divino.*" Again, the Lutherans said, "our Church cannot recognize any essential difference, *de jure divino*, of aim and authority between the two or three orders into which the ministry of grace may have been divided, *jure humano*, for the benefit and convenience of the Church."† But again the Anglicans said the Church of Sweden "has a true conception of the episcopal office." This seeming contradiction puzzled me, and in my conversation with Dr. William Tighe of Muhlenberg College I asked him why he thought the Anglicans would have accepted this Lutheran position of the Swedes as correct. He responded; "For a long time, in fact, I have wondered about the basis on which the 1920 Lambeth Conference recognized 'Swedish Orders' and whether it was based on mistaken historical information, or

---

* http://anglicanhistory.org/lutherania/conference1909.html

† Ibid.

on a non Anglo-Catholic view of episcopacy and Orders."* He speculated that, "Of course, it may be that some of the Anglican bishops in 1920 who made the decision, or who promoted it, believed in episcopacy merely as a principle of church order or government, without any regard to 'apostolic succession,' although I find this difficult to believe, or perhaps they were simply 'ignoring the details' and 'hoping for the best' in a typically middle-of-the-road Anglican way."† Given Dr. Tighe's deep knowledge of the subject, I think his opinion has weight. It would seem that both the Anglicans and the Swedish Lutherans agreed to play a game of pretend with regard to the office of bishop in order to further their ecumenical goals. But whatever the reasons, the Church of England has recognized "Swedish Orders" ever since.

This mutual recognition of orders continued throughout the twentieth century. And there were other agreements between the Anglicans and Lutherans of various countries. More Nordic and Baltic Lutherans reached levels of agreement and this culminated in the Porvoo Agreement in 1996. And in this agreement at Porvoo we see that the Anglicans and Lutherans have continued and strengthened their game of pretend that is so typical of ecumenical endeavors. At Porvoo, the participants declared: "a church which has preserved the sign of historic episcopal succession is free to acknowledge an authentic episcopal ministry in a church which has preserved continuity in the episcopal office by an occasional priestly/presbyterial ordination at the time of the Reformation."‡ Essentially, "apostolic succession" conceived of as an unbroken line of bishops consecrating each other, is, for ecumenical purposes, suspended at Porvoo. So, we see once again that the Anglicans have decided, by fiat, that all the Lutherans at Porvoo have "apostolic succession"

* Personal correspondence

† Ibid.

‡ Porvoo Common Statement, paragraph 52.

regardless of any of those silly historical details of what the Lutherans intended to do.

> [E]ach church has maintained an orderly succession of episcopal ministry within the continuity of its pastoral life, focused in the consecrations of bishops and in the experience and witness of the historic sees (IV C).
>
> In the light of all this we find that the time has come when all our churches can affirm together the value and use of the sign of the historic episcopal succession (IV D). This means that those churches in which the sign has at some time not been used are free to recognise the value of the sign and should embrace it without denying their own apostolic continuity. This also means that those churches in which the sign has been used are free to recognise the reality of the episcopal office and should affirm the apostolic continuity of those churches in which the sign of episcopal succession has at some time not been used.*

Quite a gift for the Lutherans here at Porvoo. The intellectual gyrations of the ecumenists are interesting to watch. The Anglicans are so desperate to have their ecumenical dreams realized that they delude themselves on the nature of the Swedish episcopacy. This is quite some length to go to, given that the episcopate is one of the most important things in Anglican identity. And the Swedes were desperate for ecumenical unity, as well, and for it, they would throw overboard their Confessions, and adopt an Anglican "apostolic succession."

---

* Porvoo Common Statement, paragraph 56b-57.

CONCLUSION

How does all of this affect us in the ELDoNA? Since we are trying to construct an episcopal structure within a confessional Lutheran framework, we ought to distinguish a genuine Lutheran episcopacy from ecumenically-inspired, "high-church" conceptions of episcopacy. And, to return to the title of this paper, how do confessional Lutherans view call and consecration to the episcopal office? The Swedish Church is a useful guide for us (at least from 1593 until 1904). The Swedish Church clearly practiced a consecration/ ordination type of placing bishops-elect into their office. If we in the ELDoNA are trying to construct a genuine Lutheran episcopacy, this Swedish practice would not be a bad model for us. The Swedes clearly consecrated their bishops, but just as clearly understood that the office of bishop was a grade (*jure humano*) of the one office of the ministry.

Now, how can those two things—consecration of bishops and a unitary ordination—be reconciled? Perhaps we can view this consecration as an extension of the one ordination that all ministers receive as they enter the office. We can think of it as a multi-faceted consecration, the same way men receive multiple or multi-faceted calls. A man who is being placed into the office of bishop receives a genuine consecration, but it is not in essence different or even separate (except in time) from the consecration he received when he first became a presbyter. In the episcopal consecration, our Lord God is petitioned to give the grace of the Holy Ghost to the bishop, that is, through the Holy Ghost give the gift of the office to the bishop-elect. But this office is not different than the one the man already has. It is simply an extension of that same office in a different grade.

Consecration for confessional Lutherans is necessarily self-referential. We cannot seek to have a consecration that meets with Roman or Anglican definitions or approval.

We are constrained by our Confessions to have a different understanding of consecration. An unbroken string of episcopal consecrations from some ancient starting point is a bit of *adiaphora* if considered in a vacuum, but "apostolic succession" according to a Roman or Anglican conception is not only *adiaphora* in our ecumenical world, but it is a virus that undermines our confession of a unitary office of the ministry.

I believe that as we sift through the romanticism of the sign of the episcopacy, and through the delusions of ecumenism, we are left with a self-referential consecration for Lutheran bishops. I suggest that we should practice episcopal consecration, with the laying on of hands, prayer for the gift of the Holy Ghost, and episcopal vestments, but not seek to conform our practice to the standards of the Roman or Anglican "historic episcopacy." May our Lord Jesus Christ continue to guide the Evangelical Lutheran Diocese of North America in the path of truth.

Soli Deo Gloria.

Appendix 1: Charter of the ELDoNA

In the Name of the Father and of the Son and of the Holy Ghost. Amen.

Preamble

In the book of Amos, the Lord confronted Israel with the question: "Can two walk together, unless they are agreed?" (3:3) Too often men have attempted to accomplish unity through their own works, and apart from unity in the Word of God. Thus we rejoice in the doctrinal unity which the Holy Spirit creates and sustains within the Bride of Christ, and endeavor "to keep the unity of the Spirit in the bond of peace. There is one body and one Spirit, just as you were called in one hope of your calling; one Lord, one faith, one baptism; one God and Father of all, who is above all, and through all, and in you all." (Eph. 4:3–6)

Therefore, it is our intention to give expression to the unity which the Holy Spirit has accomplished among us, and to stand together against all the snares of the evil one, and remember our brethren who are suffering in the world. (1 Pet. 5:9) As those whom Christ Jesus has called to serve Him through service to His Bride as "stewards of the mysteries of God," (1 Cor. 4:1), we expressed our unity in service by establishing *The Evangelical Lutheran Diocese of North America* on 6 June A. D. 2006. We take this step because it is our desire to "Let all things be done decently and in order."

(1 Cor. 14:40) We also called the Rev. James D. Heiser on this date to serve in the Office of Bishop and he accepted this call on 7 June 2006.

Holy Scripture and our Confessional Subscription

As Evangelical Lutherans, "We believe, teach and confess that the only rule and standard according to which at once all dogmas and teachers should be esteemed and judged are nothing else than the prophetic and apostolic Scriptures of the Old and of the New Testament..." (FC Ep. Introduction:1) Therefore we gladly reaffirm and confess "that the Unaltered Augsburg Confession is a true exposition of the Word of God and a correct exhibition of the doctrine of the Evangelical Lutheran Church" and that the entirety of the Book of Concord (1580) is "in agreement with this one Scriptural faith." (Agenda, p. 106–7) According to the intention of the formulators of Concord, we also affirm concerning the Book of Concord: "we have a unanimously received, definite, common form of doctrine, which our Evangelical churches together and in common confess; from and according to which, because it has been derived from God's Word, all other writings should be judged and adjusted as to how far they are to be approved and accepted." (FC SD Summary:10)

In keeping with this common confession, we subscribe the Niles Theses (revised 6 June A.D. 2006) and the Malone Theses (6 June A.D. 2006) not as confessional documents in themselves, but with the understanding that they are faithful to the teaching of Holy Scripture and our Lutheran Confession and address matters of concern to us as we seek to faithfully uphold our common confession in the face of the issues which trouble the Church in this generation. It is our intention that we will further address such matters in the future, and we remain open to review of these Theses where they might be stated more clearly, but in all things we seek to remain faithful to Holy Scripture and the Lutheran Confessions.

The Episcopate and the Diocese

As Evangelical Lutherans, we believe, teach and confess: "it is our greatest wish to maintain Church polity and the grades in the Church, even though they have been made by human authority" (AP XIV:24).

Therefore we have affirmed in the Malone Theses: "We recognize that a truly Evangelical Episcopacy is set forth as the preferred polity of the Evangelical Lutheran Church as taught in the Augsburg Confession (XXVIII), the Apology (XXVIII), and the Treatise on the Power and Primacy of the Pope," and "We seek the restoration of the historic, preferred polity—that is, the office of Bishop, Presbyter, and Deacon—within the one divinely-established office of the ministry as local circumstances warrant."

It is thus our intention in establishing this diocese to reestablish a position of oversight among us. As the term 'diocese' refers to an administrative area, so we desire that one would conduct such administration among us, for the sake of good order. We acknowledge that the titles "Superintendent" and "Bishop" were utilized throughout the Evangelical Lutheran Church from the time of the Reformation to designate one who had been called to the responsibility of oversight within the Church. Beginning with the Saxon Visitation of

1528, the Superintendent or Bishop was charged with the responsibility of conducting "visitations" so that "in these parishes there is correct Christian teaching, that the Word of God and the holy gospel are truly and purely proclaimed, and that the holy sacraments according to the institution of Christ are provided to the blessing of the people." (*AE* 40:313)

When Dr. Martin Chemnitz was called to the Superintendency of Braunschweig, he set forth several points regarding the office of superintendent which are pleasing to us: First, "just as we preach and teach the positive points in the one Spirit, so we will all fight on the same side in necessary controversies and stand together against errors, and when new conflicts arise, we will not each follow his own judgment and personal opinion but rather will deliberate together in conference over the points under controversy"; Second, "Likewise, we must all stick together, as we have in the past, and retain the practice that each does not build up himself or act as lord in his congregation and do what he pleases in preaching, administration of the sacraments, liturgical practices, discipline and other aspects of his office"; Third, "there must be no belittling or speaking evil of one another, but rather when some complaint arises, the matter must be put before the conference and settled while the meeting is still in session"; and Fourth, "If [the Superintendent] notices something pertaining to the office or life in a brother, [he] must speak about it either privately or before the whole conference, gently and with brotherly seriousness, and the brethren must not treat this with disdain or anger but accept it in humility. Likewise, if a brother finds some fault or failure in [the Superintendent] or the conduct of his office or life, he shall treat him in the same way." (Adapted from *The Second Martin*, p. 134–5)

Therefore, we pledge ourselves to work together in the diocese as follows:

1) We shall stand together to uphold those principles which Dr. Chemnitz affirmed regarding the Superintendency.

2) We will welcome the Bishop to conduct Visitations on a regular basis—preferably annually. During such Visitations, we will give sufficient opportunity for the Bishop to examine our doctrine and practice, and for conversation between the Bishop and the congregations we serve. We will encourage the congregations entrusted to our care to defray the Bishop's expenses connected with such Visitations.

3) We acknowledge that although each pastor does possess "by divine law" (Treatise 65) the authority to ordain ministers in his own parish, for the sake of good order we will not henceforth so ordain without the agreement of the Bishop, and we shall endeavor to express our unity by having the Bishop perform all ordinations and installations within the diocese, except as he shall otherwise authorize.

4) Admission to membership in the diocese:

a) The Bishop shall have the responsibility of examining the doctrine and life of all ordained applicant for membership in the diocese.

b) Upon completion of such examination, the Bishop shall decline such candidates as are unsuitable on the basis of doctrine or life (e.g., were previously removed from the ministry for sufficient cause).

c) The Bishop shall forward to the diocese the name and pertinent information regarding suitable candidates. (Such notification may occur by e-mail, or by surface mail.)

If the Bishop does not receive any written objections to the candidate within thirty (30) days of such notification of the diocese, the candidate shall be admitted to the diocese.

d) If a member of the diocese objects in writing to the application of a candidate, the member shall state the ground for his objection in terms of the candidate's doctrine and/or life. Such objections shall be investigated by the Bishop and two (2) other pastors or ordained deacons (whose names shall be drawn by lot). If the objections are found to be lacking merit, the candidate shall be admitted to the diocese. If the objections are substantiated, and found substantial enough to preclude the candidate's service in the diocese, the candidate shall be declined membership.

5) Discipline of members of the diocese:

a) We acknowledge that the Bishop has the responsibility of oversight among us, and has the responsibility to investigate charges of false doctrine or immoral life where such doctrine and life are either public or manifest, or when they are affirmed by the testimony of two or more witnesses.

b) We acknowledge that upon such investigation, if the Superintendent/Bishop determines that the charges are accurate, he will admonish the member of the diocese to repent and amend.

c) We acknowledge that the Bishop has the authority to suspend the membership of any pastor or ordained deacon of the diocese if the charges are substantiated, and that he will give a report to the diocese of any such suspension. If the suspended pastor does not challenge his suspension in writing to the Bishop within thirty (30) days of written notification, he shall be considered removed from the diocese.

d) if the suspended member appeals his suspension, a review panel shall be formed consisting of the Bishop and two (2) other pastors or ordained deacons of the diocese, whose names shall be drawn by lot, and shall not include the suspended member. If, upon review of the charges, the review panel determines that the substance of the charges is accurate, and that removal of the suspended member from the membership of the diocese is warranted, the suspended member shall be removed from the diocese.

e) We acknowledge and affirm that such a removal from the diocese does not remove a man from his call; congregations shall be encouraged to follow their congregational constitutions and bylaws in all such matters.

6) We acknowledge that the office of Bishop is a called office, and a 'grade' within the one office of the holy ministry. As such, there is no 'term' of office; rather, a Bishop shall serve until such time as he resigns, is called to glory, or is removed from office for cause, on the basis of false doctrine or immoral life.

7) In the event that a charge of false doctrine or immoral life is brought against the Bishop on the basis of the testimony of two or more members of the diocese, the matter shall be examined by a panel of three pastors of the diocese, whose names shall be drawn by lot. In the event that the panel substantiates the charges, and determines that they are sufficient for removal from office, the Bishop shall be removed from office, but not from membership in the diocese. Rather, such action will follow the procedure set forth in 5), after election of a new Bishop.

8) It is the responsibility of the Bishop to serve as chairman of all meetings or synods of the diocese. We pledge ourselves the intention to meet in synod annually, at a time and location determined by the Bishop, who shall make such determinations after seeking the advice and counsel of the pastors of the diocese.

9) We request that the Bishop would offer counsel to us—individually and as a diocese—so that we would work toward a greater unity of practice. Such counsel shall be considered fraternal encouragement.

We affirm that these points set forth above may be amended, or added to, by agreement of the Bishop and two-thirds of the members of the diocese during a regular synod of the diocese.

All members of *The Evangelical Lutheran Diocese of North America* pledge themselves to abide by this charter, and to conduct themselves in their relationship to the diocese and its members according to it.

Appendix 2: Points of Agreement on Controverted issues of the Day Agreed in Niles, Michigan

21 July A.D. 2005;
Amended: 6 June A.D. 2006

We all agree:

Office of the Ministry

1) The office of the ministry is not merely a function in the church but the divinely established office in the church. Its holders represent Christ to the church and give God's gifts to God's people.

2) The office of the ministry is not derived from baptism; rather it is conferred through call and ordination within the church.

3) That women cannot hold the office of the ministry, nor presume to function in it, in the church catholic.

4) Ordination is not an adiaphoron. It is part of a right understanding of a proper call.

Pulpit and Altar Fellowship

5) The practice of closed communion is biblical and confessional, and the true practice of Christian love.

6) Worship together with non-Christians is a violation of the Christian faith and a gross sin against the triune God.

7) Participation in an event of joint public prayer, that is, taking part in a religious service in which many different gods are invoked is participation in universalistic worship and is clear violation of scripture.

8) Calling such participation acceptable because it is "serial" is deceptive and a violation of scripture.

9) Being in pulpit and altar fellowship with any particular member of the Lutheran World Federation, or any other such organization, puts one in fellowship with all members of the LWF or any other such organization.

The Lord's Supper

10) The use of grape juice or any other element but natural wine for the blood of Christ in the Lord's Supper is a violation of Christ's institution, as is the use of anything other than natural bread for the body of Christ.

11) We recognize that it is preferable from the scriptures, confessions, and catholic practice that pastors offer the Lord's Supper to the flock each Lord's day, and that the divine service of word and sacrament is the normal service for the Lord's day.

Catholicity

12) The term "catholic" is not the possession of any particular church body, including the Church of Rome. To say that the church is "catholic" is to confess that it is the one true and universal church, which teaches the Word of God in

its truth and purity and administers the Sacraments according to Christ's institution. Therefore any church body which teaches false doctrines and/or corrupts the sacraments, even if it claims catholicity, is not catholic.

13) The teaching of the Unaltered Augsburg Confession (i.e. that of all the Concordia) is the true catholic doctrine. The church that faithfully adheres to and confesses this historic, apostolic faith, drawn from the unchanging Holy Scriptures, is a truly catholic church. To be truly Lutheran is to be truly catholic.

14) The Lutheran Church continues to express its catholicity through our use of the liturgy of the Western Church, as it was purified at the time of the Reformation, traditional vestments for the divine service and various prayer offices, and retention of the historic church year.

15) The Bible is God's Word without error.

Appendix 3:
The Malone Theses

Agreed to:
06 June A. D. 2006

In the Name of the Father, and of the Son, and of the Holy Ghost. Amen.

Building upon the Niles Theses of A.D. 2005, we, the undersigned, wish to further clarify our common beliefs concerning controverted issues facing the Evangelical Lutheran Church in our day. We all agree that these stated positions are our firmly held convictions, and in conformity with Holy Scripture and the Lutheran Confessions, and we wish to have fellowship with all others who teach and confess the same.

LITURGY

It is our desire to see Lutherans adopt a more fully liturgical, sacramental, and historic divine service. We wish to promote a more truly catholic practice among the saints entrusted to our care, and clearly distinguish ourselves from the 'Protestantizing' practices which dominate so much of the American Lutheran church. Therefore, we all agree that:

1) We seek to achieve a high degree of uniformity in the liturgical expression of our theological agreement among the parishes of our signators. Significant deviation in liturgical practice between parishes is confusing to the members of the

Church. Therefore, we commit ourselves to endeavor over time, by common consensus, to minimize local deviations from common practice.

2) We recognize that Lutherans in other countries observe different elements in the rite of the divine service. Lutherans in traditionally Eastern Orthodox lands may have different liturgical traditions from Lutherans in the West. However, we reject any effort to institute Eastern elements which would violate Formula of Concord article 10, that is, which give the appearance of doctrinal unity where no such unity exists.

OFFICE OF THE MINISTRY

It is our desire to fully re-establish the confessional understanding of the office of the ministry within the Lutheran Church. Therefore, we reject all 'functionalist' misconceptions of the office of the ministry. Therefore, we all agree that:

3) Laymen ought not preach or read sermons at the divine service. Laymen are not to administer the sacraments of the Church. Emergency baptism is the only exception to this rule. (AC 14)

4) The Church, corporately, possesses the office of the ministry. Our Lord Jesus Christ gave the office of the keys to the whole Church. That office is conferred upon men by the Church through call and ordination.

EPISCOPACY

It is our desire to conform ourselves to the dominant practice of the Church throughout all time on the issue of polity. We wish to distinguish ourselves from the democratic mind-set that is dominant in the Lutheran churches in America. It is the overwhelming witness of the church catholic that Episcopacy has been the accepted polity in the Church. Therefore, we all agree that:

5) We recognized that a truly Evangelical Episcopacy is set forth as the preferred polity of the Evangelical Lutheran Church as taught in the Augsburg Confession (XXVIII), the Apology (XXVIII), and the Treatise on the Power and Primacy of the Pope.

6) We seek the restoration of the historic, preferred polity—that is, the offices of Bishop, Presbyter, and Deacon—within the one divinely-established office of the ministry as local circumstances warrant.

NOMENCLATURE

The variations in terminology used to refer to occupants of the ministry and various lay officers in congregations has led to increasing confusion on the Church. While there is no law to be made regarding the terminology by which we reference offices and officeholders not established by God's Word, uniformity of usage would contribute to the teaching and preservation of correct doctrine throughout the Church. Therefore, we agree that:

7) We will endeavor to use terminology/nomenclature in the same way both in our teaching and in our parish structure.

INFANT COMMUNION

As pastors, we take seriously our responsibility to serve as "stewards of the mysteries of God." No matter how 'interesting' and 'clever' new theories may be, we reject and avoid practices that are completely unknown to the history and practice of the Church of the Augsburg Confession. Therefore, we all agree that:

8) We reject the practice of infant communion. We reject the practice of the Eastern churches which commune infants at the time of baptism. We also reject the practice of communing small children who have not been examined and absolved. We hold to article 25 of the Augsburg Confession, which says, "The custom has been retained among us of not administering the sacrament to those who have not previously been examined and absolved."

9) We reject infant communion because it undermines the pastoral responsibility to examine those who present themselves for communion. It also does not help the communicant learn the practice of self-examination. We further reject it because it has no Lutheran precedent. And finally, the erosion of pastoral examination of communicants involved in infant communion is the same as that erosion caused by the practice of open communion.

10) We also encourage the maintenance of, or restoration into our parishes of, private confession and absolution (AC XI) as a helpful practice in preparation for reception of the sacrament.

IMAGES

It has become sadly evident that there is a need to make a clear distinction between the doctrine and practices of the Evangelical Lutheran Church and the churches of Eastern Orthodoxy. Our fellowship eschews any appearance of "Easternizing." Therefore, we all agree that:

11) We reject the teaching that icons or statues or any sort of image are means of grace.

12) We, as Lutherans, embrace images as tools for piety and aids in the honoring and worship of our Lord Jesus Christ. They are also valuable tools in honoring of the saints. Images—especially the crucifix—have always been an important part of the life of the Church.

13) We recognize that in the Western Church, statuary and paintings have been an important part of the life of the Church. We encourage the use of statuary and paintings in the Church in order that they may help draw the Christian's mind to our Lord and His grace.

14) We recognize the recent use of Eastern style icons in the worship life of the Lutheran Church as an alien element in Western Lutheran churches. We reject the veneration of icons or images in the Lutheran Church.

15) We agree with the conclusions of the Blessed Martin Chemnitz regarding the Seventh Ecumenical Council and its advocacy of adoring images. He condemned this council's decree on adoration of images, whether icons or other types of images: "The chief point is that at this synod it was decreed, contrary to the clear statement of Scripture, and contrary to the unanimous testimony of all antiquity, that sacred images are to be honored, venerated, saluted, embraced, kissed, worshiped, and adored." (Ex. pp. 115-116.)

These theses, and those agreed to in Niles, Michigan are not seen by us as additions to our vows to the Scriptures and the Lutheran Confessions, which vows are unconditional. These theses may change as the issues are further clarified. However, we do see them as defining the limits of our fellowship with regard to these issues until such time as we are convinced otherwise from the Scriptures and Lutheran Confessions, or until further clarification is needed. We are keenly aware of the fluid nature of such statements. We are also keenly aware of the clear lines of distinction they draw among those who call themselves Lutherans, and we intend to draw such lines.

Many of the matters addressed by these theses are not matters that are divisive of fellowship (episcopacy, liturgy, etc.). We, in our fellowship, voluntarily agree to abide by these theses for the well being of our parishes. These theses are not a declaration of fellowship. Those inside our fellowship voluntarily agree with these theses and support them. But we also wish to have these theses function as a marker of agreement between Christians who are not yet necessarily in fellowship. Therefore, we invite all who agree with these theses to express their agreement without necessarily committing themselves to fellowship.

We hope and pray that these theses will be yet another building block in establishing a more healthy and orthodox Lutheran Church in our time, and in this country. With this hope, we with joy and profound thanks to our triune God, accept and confess these theses.

The Rite of Consecration to the Office of Bishop appointed for use in The Evangelical Lutheran Diocese of North America

The Consecration of the Rt. Rev. James D. Heiser
as Bishop of the ELDoNA.
Called to the grade of bishop the sixth of June, A.D. 2006,
consecrated this sixteenth day of May, A.D. 2010.

Rev. C. D. Hudson, *Ordinarius*
Rev. Jeffrey Ahonen, and
Rev. John Rutowicz, assisting

THE RITE OF EPISCOPAL CONSECRATION

Procession
Crucifer
Book Bearers
Clergy of the Diocese
Assisting Clergy
Bishop
Ordinarius

Hymn *Come, Holy Ghost, God and Lord, TLH 224*

Exhortation
Ordinarius: Dear friends, let us pray Almighty God our Heavenly Father, for all our necessities, and especially that He vouchsafe to this man here present, who is elected to the Office of Bishop, His holy grace, that he may so execute this office, that it may be pleasing unto Him, and fruitful and profitable to the people who are entrusted to his care.

The Litany
All The Litany, TLH 661

Collects *Litany Collect, TLH p 112; Collect for the Church #16, TLH p 103*

Ordinarius: Let us pray: Almighty God, Who knowest us to be set in the midst of so many and great dangers that by reason of the frailty of our nature we cannot always stand upright, grant us such strength and protection as may support us in all dangers and carry us through all temptations; through Jesus Christ, Thy Son, our Lord, Who liveth and

reigneth with Thee and the Holy Ghost, ever one God, world without end.
All: Amen.

Ordinarius: *Almighty and Gracious God,* the Father of our Lord Jesus Christ, Who hast commanded us to pray that Thou wouldst send forth laborers into Thy harvest, of Thine infinite mercy give us true teachers and ministers of Thy Word, and put Thy saving Gospel in their hearts and on their lips that they may truly fulfill Thy command and preach nothing contrary to Thy Holy Word, that we, being warned, instructed, nurtured, comforted and strengthened by Thy Heavenly Word, may do those things which are well-pleasing to Thee and profitable to us; through Jesus Christ, Thy Son, our Lord, Who liveth and reigneth with Thee and the Holy Ghost, ever one God, world without end.
All: Amen.

Lection
Lector 1 Timothy 3:1-7
Lector Acts 20:28-31
Lector St. Luke 12:42-48

Response to each reading:
V *But Thou, O Lord, have mercy upon us.*
R *Thanks be to Thee, O Lord.*

Exposition and Affirmations
Ordinarius In these words, our dear Lord Jesus Christ doth clearly declare unto us:
First, that they that are called to such an office as the Bishop's, have obtained a commission from God, not over some

small concerns, but over His people and servants; yea, them hath He purchased and redeemed with His own blood, that they should bestow upon them that which is required by their necessity; that is, that they should provide them with the word of eternal life, through which they
can have refreshment and strength.

Then next we hear also that God requireth of them two things; the one is faithfulness, the other is ability and understanding. Faithfulness maketh them to to be diligent; ability that they know how to undertake their commission.

For the third, we also hear what reward is promised to them, when they carry out their commission well; namely that they shall have authority over all that belongeth to our Lord Jesus Christ. On the other hand we hear also what awaiteth them if they conduct themselves otherwise than they ought in this office; namely, everlasting punishment with all unfaithful servants. Therefore shall this word of our Lord Jesus Christ ever abide in our minds, and awaken us that we be not negligent herein nor assuredly offend, but in all respects prove ourselves good, faithful, and sensible servants.

Q Which if thou also with God's help wilt do, say, Yea.
A Yea.

Q Wilt thou in the Name of God the Holy Trinity undertaketh this ministry and office of Bishop?
A Yea.

Q Wilt thou apply thyself thereunto, that it may rightly

and worthily be exercised to the glory of God and the good of His Church?

A Yea.

Q Wilt thou also at all times remain in the pure Word of God [and the Book of Concord of 1580 as a faithful exhibition of the pure Word of God] and flee all false and heretical doctrine?

A Yea.

Q Wilt thou likewise so order thy life that thou set a good example and give no cause for scandal?

A Yea.

Q Confess thy faith

A *Recitation of the Nicene Creed*

Ordinarius The Lord God strengthen and comfort thee hereunto and to every good thing.

Amen.

Responsorium

Consecration

The Bishop kneels

Ordinarius and other participating pastors lay hands on the head of ordinandus

Ordinarius Let us pray:

All Pastors The Lord's Prayer

Ordinarius O Everlasting and Merciful God, dear Heavenly Father who, through the mouth of Thy dearly beloved Son Jesus Christ, hast taught us 'The harvest is great, but the laborers are few. Pray, therefore, the Lord of the harvest that He would send laborers into His harvest.' With which words He gives us to understand, that we cannot elsewhere receive orthodox and faithful teachers than of Thy gentle hand. We, therefore, beseech Thee heartily, that Thou wouldest mercifully look upon this Thy servant whom we have chosen and taken to this service and Bishop's office, giving him Thy Holy Spirit, that he may truly and powerfully carry out Thy holy work, teach and rebuke with all meekness and wisdom. So that Thy holy gospel may always remain among us pure and without falsehood, and bear us the fruit of salvation and eternal life. Through Thy Son Jesus Christ our Lord. Amen.

Ordinarius By the authority which is entrusted to me, on God's behalf, by His Church for this purpose, I commit to thee the Bishop's office, in the Name of the Father and of the Son and of the Holy Ghost. Amen.

Ordinarius Wait on the LORD: be of good courage, and he shall strengthen thine heart: wait, I say, on the LORD. (Psalm 27:14)

Vestment and Enthronement

As the hymn is sung, the Bishop is dressed with cope and miter and is handed the crozier; he then takes his chair.

Hymn *We Now Implore God the Holy Ghost, TLH 231*

The Divine Service continues at TLH p. 15

Concerning this Rite of Consecration

The Evangelical Lutheran Diocese of North America (ELDoNA) has, from its very inception, desired to re-establish the historic episcopal polity of the Lutheran Church within its midst. In June of 2006 the ELDoNA was established, and in that same synod the members of the ELDoNA elected Pastor James D. Heiser as the bishop of the diocese. This was his call to the bishop's office, and he began to function in that office immediately. The members of the ELDoNA have been pleased to call Pastor Heiser their bishop over the last four years recognizing that the most essential element of his being a bishop had been fulfilled, namely his call to that office. However, it has been recognized since the very beginning that it was not advisable to continue on indefinitely without completing all the elements of his call, that is, his consecration as bishop. We, the members of the ELDoNA, did not worry about the episcopal consecration at first because as Lutherans we understand that the office of bishop is simply one grade in the one divinely established office of the ministry. Bishop Heiser was already ordained into the one office of the ministry and could function in any grade of the office of the ministry by virtue of his original ordination. But that all things might be done in good order, the members of ELDoNA called him to this new grade of office, and now consecrate him in that new office. One might think of this call and consecration of the bishop as an extension of his original call and ordination, but to a new grade or realm of responsibility. He is recognized as first among equals. With the completion of this episcopal consecration the ELDoNA will have completely achieved its desire to re-establish the bishop's office in its midst.

The consecration rite that is celebrated today is almost exactly the same consecration rite that was created by Archbishop Laurentius Petri in 1571. Laurentius Petri was the first Lutheran Archbishop of Sweden. He and his brother Olavus are considered the fathers of the Lutheran Reformation in Sweden as Martin Luther and Philip Melanchthon are in Germany. Archbishop Petri created this rite of consecration specifically for the Lutheran Church in Sweden and so it can be considered a thoroughly and completely Lutheran rite. Archbishop Petri also has a reputation of impeccable orthodoxy so that his writings are supremely trustworthy. The ELDoNA is using his rite today almost completely. In the few spots where the rite was incomplete for our purposes we added parts from Martin Luther's 1542 rite for the consecration of bishops.

www.ingramcontent.com/pod-product-compliance
Lightning Source LLC
Chambersburg PA
CBHW071618040426
42452CB00009B/1381

9781891469466